FOREWORD

THE exhibition of German expressionism arranged jointly by the Folkwang Museum in Essen and the Art Gallery of New South Wales, adds one more building block to the magnificent edifice of cultural exchange between our two countries; it presents the opportunity to get to know at first hand one of the major trends in 20th century German painting which produced both such distinguished groups of artists as "Die Brücke" and "Der Blau Reiter", and prominent individual painters such as Emil Nolde and Max Beckmann. Expressionism is not simply a chapter of German art history; its decisive influence on the development of 20th century painting has been felt throughout the whole world.

At the same time, the fate of German expressionism and its artists is part of Germany's bitter past. Expressionism was at odds with the heroizing, racist taste in art prescribed by the National Socialists. Between 1933 and 1945 it was derided, condemned and persecuted as "degenerate art", banned from museums and sold off abroad. Its artists were forbidden to paint; many went into exile; some faced wretched circumstances.

Thus the exhibition also represents an attempt to make amends to those who were persecuted and to their great works of art.

This exhibition does not merely display major art works of this century. It also reflects a period of political history. It reminds us of the importance of freedom, the lifeblood of all art.

Dr Barthold C. Witte
Director General for Cultural Relations
Federal Foreign Office, Bonn
Federal Republic of Germany

GERMAN EXPRESSIONISM

First published in October 1989 by International Cultural Corporation of Australia Limited, 12 Playfair Street, The Rocks, Sydney, New South Wales, Australia, 2000.

© International Cultural Corporation of Australia Limited 1989

National Library of Australia Cataloguing-in-Publication entry:

German Expressionism
  ISBN 0 642 14786 8.

   1. Graphic arts – Germany – History – 20th century –
   Exhibitions. 2. Expressionism (Art) – Germany – Exhibitions.
   I. International Cultural Corporation of Australia

760.094307494

Designed and produced by John Witzig, Mullumbimby NSW
Printed by Griffin Press, Adelaide SA

GERMAN EXPRESSIONISM

THE COLOURS OF DESIRE

Organised by Museum Folkwang, Essen
and Art Gallery of New South Wales, Sydney
Managed by International Cultural Corporation of Australia Limited
Indemnified by the Australian Government
through the Department of the Arts, Sport, the Environment,
Tourism and Territories

Made possible by a grant from the
Government of the Federal Republic of Germany

Sponsored by
Lufthansa German Airlines and Deutsche Bank A.G.

Proudly supported by
Mercedes-Benz Pty Ltd

Carried in Australia by Australian Airlines

Exhibition Dates
11 October — 10 December, 1989
Art Gallery of New South Wales

20 December, 1989 — 18 February, 1990
National Gallery of Victoria

ACKNOWLEDGEMENTS

LENDERS TO THE EXHIBITION

Brücke-Museum, Berlin	Director:	Prof. Dr Magdalena M Moeller
Staatliche Museen Preussischer		
Kulturbesitz Nationalgalerie, Berlin	Director:	Prof. Dr Deiter Honisch
Städtisches Kunstmuseum, Bonn	Director:	Dr Katharina Schmidt
Kunsthalle, Bremen	Director:	Dr Siegfried Salzmann
Museum am Ostwall, Dortmund	Director:	Dr Ingo Bartsch
Leopold-Hoesch-Museum der Stadt, Duren	Director:	Dr Dorothea Eimert
Kunstmuseum, Dusseldorf	Director:	Dr Hans A. Peters
Museum Folkwang, Essen	Director:	Dr Georg-W Költzsch
Städtisches Museum Gelsenkirchen, Gelsenkirchen-Buer	Director:	Dr Reinhold Lange
Karl Ernst Osthaus Museum, Hagen	Director:	Dr Michael Fehr
Sprengel-Museum, Hannover	Director:	Prof. Dr Joachim Buchner
Städtisches Museum, Mulheim	Director:	Dr Karin Stempel
Bayerische Staatsgemäldesammlungen, Munich	Director:	Prof. Dr Hubertus Falkner von Sonnenburg
Städtische Galerie im Lenbachhaus, Munich	Director:	Dr Armin Zweite
Westfälisches Landesmuseum für Kunst und Kulturgeschichte, Munster	Director:	Prof. Dr Klaus Bussmann
Städtische Kunsthalle, Recklinghausen	Director:	Dr Ferdinand Ullrich
Galerie der Stadt, Stuttgart	Director:	Dr Johann-Karl Schmidt
Staatsgalerie Stuttgart	Director:	Prof. Dr Peter Beye
Art Gallery of New South Wales, Sydney	Director:	Edmund Capon
Private Collection, Federal Republic of Germany		

EXHIBITION ORGANISATION

FEDERAL REPUBLIC OF GERMANY
Museum Folkwang, Essen
Director: Dr Georg-W. Költzsch
Former Director: Prof. Dr Paul Vogt

AUSTRALIA
Art Gallery of New South Wales, Sydney
Director: Edmund Capon

EXHIBITION MANAGEMENT

International Cultural Corporation of Australia Limited

ASSISTANCE TO THE EXHIBITION AND BOOK

Prof. Dr Lorenz Dittmann, Professor of Art History, University of Saarland
Dr Hubertus Froning, Chief Curator, Museum Folkwang, Essen
Prof. Dr Magdalena M. Moeller, Director of the Brücke Museum, Berlin
Dr Olaf Reinhardt, University of New South Wales
Dr Barthold C. Witte, Director General for Cultural Relations, Federal Foreign Office, Bonn, Federal Republic of Germany
Dr Armin Zweite, Director of the Städtische Galerie im Lenbachhaus, Munich
Goethe Institute, Sydney

FOREWORDS

THIS exhibition is the culmination of several years planning in both the Federal Republic of Germany and Australia. It is a significant event as it is the first exhibition of German Expressionist paintings to come to Australia. We are deeply indebted to Prof. Paul Vogt, former Director, Museum Folkwang, Essen, who initiated negotiations with lenders, Mr Edmund Capon, Director, Art Gallery of New South Wales and Dr Georg Költzsch, Director, Museum Folkwang, who have chosen the works and arranged the loans. Lenders have been understandably hesitant about allowing some of their finest and often fragile works to travel. We are most grateful to them for their generosity which will enable Australians to view some of the most significant paintings from this influential period of twentieth century art.

The tour of the exhibition has been made possible by the generosity and support of the Government of the Federal Republic of Germany; particular thanks must also go to the sponsors of the exhibition.

The works in the exhibition are indemnified by the Australian Government through the Department of the Arts, Sport, the Environment, Tourism and Territories. Once again we thank them for their continuing support and co-operation.

ICCA is delighted and proud to join the Museum Folkwang and the Art Gallery of New South Wales in presenting the exhibition, "German Expressionism: The Colours of Desire".

James B. Leslie A.O, M.C
Chairman
International Cultural Corporation of Australia Limited

THE notion of a major exhibition of German Expressionist art for Australia has been in our minds for well over five years. Added impetus to the idea was provided in 1984 when the Art Gallery of New South Wales purchased Kirchner's *Three Bathers*, that Gallery's first German Expressionist painting and one which quickly took its place as an exemplary work of a movement which had such impact not only in Europe but also in Australia. Strangely, though, the art of the German Expressionists had never been shown to an Australian public in any even marginally comprehensive way. This exhibition is, therefore, in our view long overdue and very welcome.

It would not, however, have happened without the constant enthusiasm and support of, firstly, the Goethe Institute in Sydney and, secondly, the Department for Cultural Relations, Federal Foreign Office in Bonn. Once agreement in principle had been obtained, in 1987, Prof. Paul Vogt, then Director of the Museum Folkwang in Essen, was charged with overall curatorial responsibility. We owe a considerable debt of gratitude to Prof. Vogt for his work and for enlisting the support of the appropriate authorities and the proposed lending institutions in Germany. Upon his retirement as Director of Museum Folkwang in 1988 he was succeeded by Dr Georg Költzsch who also took on the responsibilities for this exhibition. I must express my thanks to Dr Költzsch and his colleagues both at the Museum Folkwang and elsewhere for their diligence and tenacity in orchestrating the loans with so many museums, just as I express my thanks to those museums and the lone private collector who have so kindly made their works available.

The number of lenders, the fragility of the paintings and the logistics in gathering the material together has placed a very considerable burden on Dr Költzsch and the Museum Folkwang staff. The successful conclusion to all these negotiations and arrangements is due to their commitment. I must also express our thanks to Dr Barthold Witte, Director General for Cultural Relations, of the Federal Foreign Office in Bonn, for his support and involvement.

Many hands and minds have contributed to the catalogue for this exhibition. We are most grateful to the four German scholars who have contributed the introductory essays which provide such a succinct but illuminating background to the schools and themes of German Expressionist art. To Dr Olaf Reinhardt of the University of New South Wales, our thanks for the translations and to the curatorial and education staff of the Art Gallery of New South Wales our thanks for their work in editing, checking and proof-reading.

On behalf of the Art Gallery of New South Wales and the National Gallery of Victoria we acknowledge as ever the management skills of the International Cultural Corporation of Australia in handling the financial and administrative responsibilities.

Finally to our sponsors, in their many guises, our grateful thanks, for without such support we would be quite unable to stage such an important exhibition. To the Federal Foreign Office in Bonn for their co-operation and financial support, to Lufthansa German Airlines for their substantial sponsorship and to the Deutsche Bank A.G. and Mercedes-Benz Pty Ltd our thanks for their financial support. To the Australian Government our gratitude for the indemnity provisions without which we would be quite unable to offer exhibitions of such significance and quality.

Edmund Capon
Director
Art Gallery of New South Wales

IT has become difficult to present the painting of German Expressionism in comprehensive exhibitions. Too many pictures have travelled too often and for too long, and too many are even now away as loans at numerous exhibition locations. Above all, it is thanks to the great understanding and special helpfulness of the lenders, that the wish, expressed by the museums in Sydney and Melbourne, to hold an Expressionism exhibition, could be fulfilled. The well-founded caution of responsible curators and restorers certainly explains why some artists are not represented in the exhibition at all (like Ludwig Meidner) or only as part of the exhibition of prints (like George Grosz). Certainly we would have liked to show a larger selection of pictures by Ernst Ludwig Kirchner, Erich Heckel or Franz Marc, in order to present particular themes even more clearly. Max Beckmann's wonderful *Frauenbad (Women's bath)* from 1919 has been borrowed; a second, earlier picture could no longer be obtained. The selection of his works therefore extends from 1919 to the late thirties, and thus clearly extends that time limit which marks the end of Expressionism, which is around 1920 – a few years after the end of the First World War. To say this, at the beginning, does not mean to deplore any shortcoming. Each exhibition, as a composition of examples, gives its own interpretation relative to its time. No exhibition was able in the past, nor will be able in the future, to represent completely and accurately the art of German Expressionism in its origin, its development and its manifold facets. And today there is also no book which offers such a valid and exhaustive representation. The phenomenon "Expressionism" is, even theoretically, not at all sufficiently developed or interpreted. The concept "Expressionism" already has too many facets to enable it to be explained in a one-dimensional way or even with the frequently used catchwords.

The exceptional quality of the hundred or so exhibited paintings and prints illustrates with necessary clarity the large scope of expressionist creative style and form. The two definite poles of the large spectrum can be seen in Dresden and Munich. When "Die Brücke" (The Bridge) was founded in Dresden in 1905, young artistic talents, who had to first search for their way into painting, came together. When the "Blaue Reiter" got its name in 1911, Kandinsky had already carried out the advance into an abstract world of images and Franz Marc had created his first large animal compositions as Utopias of a new world harmony. The Munich artists accompanied their artistic work with theoretical reflections. The Dresden artists pursued a way of living which was accentuated with hedonism. The Munich artists cultivated international contacts and were especially interested in French art. The Dresden artists vigorously rejected all influences and relied on the originality of spontaneous painting. There was no love lost between Dresden and Munich. The Munich artists did not particularly appreciate "The Wild Ones" in Dresden. The Munich artists remained in Munich. The Dresden artists went to Berlin in 1911, the year the "Blaue Reiter" had its first exhibition.

In Berlin, "Die Brücke" broke apart. From the Dresden group style, well-developed personal styles were formed, which led to a peak of expressionist painting. The cheerful nudes from the happy days at the Moritzburg lakes near Dresden, had developed, in Kirchner's work, into nervously drawn nudes and then into demi-mondaines. The place of happy girls was now being taken by the *Kranke Frau (Sick Woman)*. This sympathy with society could not be found in any of the Dresden pictures. Not even in the case of Heckel, whose *Irrenhaus (Lunatic asylum)* of 1914 described, as it were, the situation of human beings in the threatening shadow of the catastrophe of the World War. Expressionism had become different in Berlin. And in Berlin, the sultry autumn of the empire was more noticeable, more immediately present than in Munich. Even Marc's visions broke apart, but in a more detached manner, towards an order of new systems of images: striking and disciplined. In 1914, Kandinsky returned to Russia temporarily. August Macke, the friend of the "Blaue Reiter" in the Rhineland, preserved the sensuous happiness of an infinite beauty of nature. He was killed in 1914 in France, Franz Marc in 1916 at Verdun. Heckel did medical service in Belgium. Kirchner broke down physically and psychologically during service in the field and had to begin a stay at a sanatorium. At that point, in Berlin, Dix and Grosz intensified expressionist painting to yield sarcastic pictures of an unmasked society, by means of combining different expressionist creative styles and extending them with new stylistic techniques. With this, it is true, "Expressionism", or better, the expressionistic creative style, became a method of representation, whereas in Dresden and Munich (and for the "loners" between these poles), "Expressionism" was the original language of a new way of living or a spiritual equivalent for the world in images.

The awakening of Expressionism in Dresden, its different form in Munich and the radical change in Berlin, are at the same time essential historical stages and fixed points useful for orientation in the exhibition as well as in the broad spectrum of expressionist artistic and creative possibilities between 1905 and 1920.

Georg-W. Költzsch
Director of the Museum Folkwang, Essen

GERMAN EXPRESSIONISM

ON THE DEFINITION OF GERMAN EXPRESSIONISM

LORENZ DITTMANN

EXPRESSIONISM has become an apparently self-evident, generally accepted designation. Like all terms which refer to artistic styles and trends, the word "Expressionism" proves to be ambiguous and complex when examined more closely.

French writings on art brought the word "expression" into circulation around 1900. Even here, there are different nuances of meaning.[1]

"Expression" can mean "expression of self". This was postulated by the Symbolist painter Gustave Moreau, and by Paul Fist in 1899, one year after Moreau's death, as the true task of the artist.

But the word can also mean "expression of an object". It was used in this sense when the young painter André Derain wrote to his friend Maurice de Vlaminck in 1901, that a telegraph wire ought to be depicted in gigantic proportions "because it transmitted so much information".

Finally, "expression" can also mean the "expression of the picture itself". That is the sense given it by Henri Matisse in his *Notes d'un peintre* in 1908 referring to the formal structure of the painting as a whole. This kind of "expression" is "décoration" at the same time.

The word "expression" requires further definition: "expression of what?" - expression of the artist, of the object represented, or of the painting?

This need for differentiation also applies to earlier uses of the term "expression" - for the word is of course not an invention of the period around 1900. To quote but two examples from older theories of art:

In 1715, the French painter Charles le Brun published a *Conférence sur l'expression générale et particulier des passions* (Lecture on the general and particular expression of the passions), in which he uses "expression" to mean mainly the "caractère de chaque chose" (the nature of each thing), that is, the expression of the object.

The French theoretician and critic Roger de Piles, in his *Cours de Peinture* (Course on painting) of 1708, was already using "expression" in its subjective meaning; he meant "la pensée du cœur humain" (the thought of the human heart).[2]

The person regarded as the greatest exemplar of artistic self-expression was Michelangelo. As late as 1855, Jacob Burckhardt wrote about Michelangelo in his *Cicerone*: "The signature of the last three centuries, subjectivity, appears here in the form of an absolutely unrestricted creativity. But it does not do this unintentionally and unconsciously as is the case in so many of the great spiritual movements of the sixteenth century, but with a powerful intention..."[3]

"Self-expression", the term with which we began and ended our brief survey, thus appears to be at the centre of meaning of the word "expression". At the same time, we saw that different values were attached to it.

In what sense was this term understood in relation to German Expressionist painting?

The earliest "Expressionist" artistic statement, the programme of the "Brücke" cut in wood by Ernst Ludwig Kirchner in 1906, concludes with the sentence: "That artist is one of us who reproduces immediately and unadulterated what it is that drives him to create." "Immediacy", "unadulterated" are thus characteristics of a specifically "Expressionist" art, but also an indication that it arises from a "drive to create".[4]

These are also the criteria Kirchner stressed in his

PROFESSOR DR LORENZ DITTMANN
Professor of Art History, University of Saarland

reviews when, under the pseudonym "Louis de Marsalle", he wrote reviews of his own works.[5] Thus, for instance he writes in a review published in 1921 entitled *On the Swiss Works of E.L. Kirchner* : "Since these paintings have been created with blood and nerves and not with coldly calculating reason, they speak to us directly and emotively. They create the impression that the painter had layered many versions of an experience one on top of the other. Despite all the calm, a fiery, passionate struggle for the objects can be felt...[6] "Experience" and "directness" are the crucial words here too, but they have been reduced to their physiological bases, to "blood and nerves" ".This kind of reduction does not occur in the writings of the Dresden art-critic Paul Fechter, later to be Max Pechstein's biographer. In his book, *Expressionism*, which appeared in Munich in 1914, he declared that the task of the observer of Expressionist works was not "to read in them what the painting 'represents', to reconstruct in the mind's eye the original picture of reality from the colour analysis of that reality; rather, it is to gain access to the feeling out of which the painting grew for the artist by the detour of what the picture provides". The aim, according to Fechter, "is no longer to gain knowledge but to feel, to ascend to those regions of the soul where slumbers the force that corresponds to the productive power which gave rise to the work...".[7]

"Feeling" is to be the bridge between the observer and the painter; the work itself is merely the medium of transmission. In this type of theoretical approach, there is no reflection on the problem of artistic structuring itself, the special nature of the "pictorial expression" as such, the experience of

ERNST LUDWIG KIRCHNER
Schlemihl's encounter with the shadow
Colour woodcut Cat. 73
Museum Folkwang, Essen

concrete expressive values in colours and shapes.

"Direct self-expression" and "feeling", however, do not suffice to characterise the new "Expressionist art" within a more comprehensive intellectual horizon. An attempt to establish the position of art as the expression of a basic attitude to the world was undertaken by Wilhelm Worringer in his thesis *Abstraction and Empathy. A contribution to the psychology of style*, which appeared in book form in 1908. It became the basic text of Expressionist art theory.[8] Worringer [9] distinguished two basic possibilities of the human "attitude to the world", the "drive to empathy" and the "drive to abstraction". The former finds its satisfaction in the "beauty of the organic"; one of its conditions is a "happy pantheistic intimacy between man and the phenomena of the external world". The "drive to abstraction", on the other hand, is "the result of a great inner disturbance of man by the phenomena of the external world and on the religious level corresponds to a strongly transcendental colouring of all ideas". This state Worringer called "a huge spiritual view of space" and added: "When Tibullus says: *primum in mundo fecit deus timor* (the first thing God made in the world was fear) this same feeling of fear can also refer to the roots of artistic creation.".

Thus the "drive to abstraction" attains its satisfaction in the "life-denying inorganic, in the crystalline, or generally, in all abstract regularity and necessity". "In the drive to abstraction, the intensity of the urge to lose oneself is incomparably greater and more consistent. Unlike the drive to empathy, which is not characterised by an urge to lose one's individual being, but as an urge to be released, by the contemplation of something necessary and immutable, from the accidental nature of human existence; from the apparent arbitrariness of organic existence in general." Worringer regarded Greek art and all so-called naturalistic art as the principal examples of empathic art, and "primitive" art, that of the Egyptians and of the early twentieth century, as the principal examples of abstract art.

In this conception, nothing remains of art as "self-expression"; on the contrary, the new art emerges from the urge "to be released, by the contemplation of something necessary and immutable, from the accidental nature of human existence altogether". This introduces a new element into the theory of Expressionist art.

In this changed form it affected the theoretical artistic reflections unifying the *Blue Rider Almanac*. This book, which appeared in 1912, was the first comprehensive explanation of modern art against the background of world art written by artists.[10] Contributions by Franz Marc, August Macke, Wassily Kandinsky, David Burljuk, Arnold Schönberg and others were accompanied by illustrations of selected works by the "Brücke"-artists, and those of the "Blue Rider" group, but also of Picasso, Robert Delaunay, El Greco, Paul Cézanne, Henri Rousseau, 15th and 16th century German woodcuts, Bavarian painted glass pictures, Japanese drawings, Russian folk-prints, carved statues from Southern Borneo, the Easter Islands, Cameroon, Mexico, New Caledonia etc.

This means that the horizon goes well beyond Worringer's theoretical-historical attempt. In a crucial contrast to Worringer's basing abstraction on fear of the world, the expositions of the artists (as already in the "Brücke"-programme) are full of the awareness of a new beginning, of the longing to set off into a new realm of liberty and of the spirit.

In Franz Marc's contribution, *The 'Fauves' of Germany* (by which he understood especially the artists of the Dresden "Brücke", the Berlin "New Secession"and the "New Artists' Association of Munich"), he turned against a purely formal interpretation of the new aspects of their art: "It is impossible to try to explain the latest works of these 'Fauves' by a formal development and re-interpretation of Impressionism ... The most beautiful prismatic colours and the famous Cubism have lost their meaning as goals for these 'Fauves'.

"Their thinking has another goal: by their work to create symbols for their time, symbols which belong on the altars of the future spiritual religions and behind which their technical procreator disappears."

"Mysticism awoke in their souls and with it, age-old elements of art."

Cézanne and El Greco are much-admired models for Marc. "The works of both stand at the entrance of a new era of painting. Both felt in their world view the mystical inner construction which is the great problem of today's generation". Marc also pointed this out in another contribution, called *Spiritual Treasures*, and his third essay, *Two Paintings*, which contains the prophetic words: "There are unconventional, fiery signs of the time increasing in all places to-day. This book is intended to be their focus until the new age dawns and, with its natural light, takes away from these works the ghostly appearance in which they are still manifest in to-day's world..."[11]

August Macke also expressed himself in a similar way. His article *Masks* centres around a new definition of form: "Form is a secret for us, because it is an expression of mysterious forces. It is only through it that we can sense the mysterious forces, the 'invisible God'. For us, the senses are the bridge from the incomprehensible to the comprehensible. Looking at plants and animals is: feeling their mystery. Hearing the thunder is: feeling its mystery. Understanding the language of forms means: being closer to the mystery, living.

"Creating forms means: life. Are not children creators who create directly out of the mystery of their feelings, more than the imitators of Greek forms? Are not the savages artists who have their own form, strong as the form of thunder?"

"Mankind gives expression to its life in forms. Every art form is an expression of inner life. The exterior of the art form is its interior."[12]

Not only "feeling" becomes visible in the work of art, but the whole "inner life" of mankind, not only the "self-expression" of the artist is precipitated in the work, but at the same time life, the forces of whatever comes together in nature, creating in this way a new relationship between man and nature.

In the centre of the *Blue Rider Almanac* stands Wassily Kandinsky's great treatise "On the Question of Form". It too is borne by the belief in the arrival of a "great spiritual epoch". As its characteristics "in present-day art" Kandinsky lists "1. a great liberty, which seems boundless to some, and which 2. makes the spirit audible, which 3. we can see reveal itself in an especially powerful force in things, which 4. will gradually take as its tool all spiritual areas and already does so, from which 5. it will create in every spiritual area, including the visual arts (especially in painting), many autonomous means of expression (forms) encompassing both individuals and groups 6. which has available to it the entire larder, i.e., every material, from the most 'solid' to that living only two-dimensionally (abstract) will be used as an element of form."

Point 6 was expounded by Kandinsky with the observation that "the forms in which it is manifest, torn from the store cupboard of matter by the spirit ... can easily be arranged between two poles". "These two poles are 1. the great abstraction, 2. the great realism. These two poles open up two paths which ultimately lead to a single goal".

With this, Kandinsky was aiming from the start for a great synthesis, for an equality of the two paths of "abstract" and "representational" art, which have unfortunately been set against each other often enough in our century.

Kandinsky proposed that what "great realism" and "great abstraction" had in common was what he called the "inner harmony". "Great realism is a striving to drive the external artistic aspects from the painting and to embody the content of the work in the simple ('non-artistic') representation of the simple hard object. The outer husk of the object conceived and fixed in the painting in this way and the simultaneous removal of its customary obtrusive beauty are the surest ways of revealing the inner harmony of the object."

"The great antithesis to this realism is the great abstraction, which consists of the endeavour, apparently to remove the concrete (real) entirely, and tries to embody the content of the work in 'non-material' forms. Abstract life, conceived and fixed in the painting in this way, reduced to a minimum of concrete forms and thus to the conspicuous predominance of abstract units, is the surest way of revealing the inner harmony of the painting."[13]

Thus Kandinsky described the "expression of the object" and the "expression of the painting" and the combination of the two methods of expression.

Kandinsky does not mention "self-expression" anywhere, but talks about the "expression of the world": "The world resounds. It is a cosmos of spiritually acting beings. It is the living spirit in dead matter."[14]

With this kind of pushing back of "self-expression" in favour of supra-personal expression, Kandinsky is thinking along the same lines as the philosopher and theoretician of art, Ludwig Coellen in his book New Painting. This appeared in 1912, the same year as the Blue Rider Almanac. Coellen distinguished Expressionism from Impressionism in the following terms: "The essential difference between the objectivism of Impressionist painting, which is also based on the concrete, and Expressionism is the dominance of the spiritual: the concrete increases its validity in the sphere of the spiritual". This "spiritual", however, is not carried by the "self", by the individuality of the artist, ie. it is not "self-expression". On the contrary, this "spiritual" actually demands the dissolution of the individual: "The law of the dissolution of individual value in favour of the spiritual energy of the totality, which is the secret and mysterious root of all individual concreteness, has suddenly become the sure dominant motif in the visualising of the most recent painters" (ie. the Expressionists).[15]

The "spiritual energy of the totality" of Coellen is comparable to the "resounding world" of Kandinsky. Both authors pointed to the fact that the artists became aware of a spiritual world encompassing them, that the works of the new Expressionist art exhaust themselves neither in self-expression nor in the expression of individual concrete objects, but are, above and beyond this, the expression of a spiritual world.

Despite this, later commentators reduced the characterisation of Expressionism to the expression of subjectivity. Thus Hans Hildebrandt declared in his lecture of 1919, Expressionism in Painting, that this had "re-erected the primacy of the inner world. Giving sensuous expression to what is alive in the creating artist" was everything for Expressionist painting.[16]

George Marzynski, in his 1920 article, *The Method of Expressionism*, stressed the subjective sphere: "Expressionist art no longer aims to sublimate the objective side of total reality but to sublimate the subject ... Expressionism remains enclosed within the realm of the subject, its objectifications are nothing more than means for extending the subject..." In addition, Marzynski tried to concretise this subjective dimension as a sphere of "imagination". Expressionist artists, he said, painted "imagination pictures". "Imagination of things" was the true basis of their paintings.[17]

However this leaves Expressionist art inadequately defined. Such is the case if it is seen only as a vehicle for the "self-expression" of artists.

Let us conclude this overview of the definitions of the term "Expressionism" in German-language art criticism between 1900 and 1920, by summarising its wealth of meanings. Its specification as the "self-expression" of the artist, as obvious as it may seem and frequently used though it was, does not suffice. It must also account for "expression of the object", "expression of the painting itself" and finally "expression of a world in total", whether this is characterised by anxiety and threat or by a new spirituality and freedom.

But a semantic analysis such as this makes only the most general scheme available for interpretation. It is only by looking at and analysing the works themselves that their special nature and inner fullness, the expressive power of the shapes and colours, their strength, spontaneity and simplicity are revealed. These are not accessible to general concepts, they can be reached only by seeing them, and the word, the concepts have to serve this seeing as well.

NOTES

1 C.f. Donald E Gordon, "On the Origin of the Word 'Expressionism'". In: *Journal of the Warburg and Courtauld Institutes,* 29, 1966, 368-385.

2 C.f. Wladislaw Tartarkiewicz, *History of Aesthetics,* Vol III: Modern Aesthetics. The Hague, Paris, Warsaw, 1974, pp.402, 404, 412, 413.

3 Jacob Burckhardt, *Gesammelte Werke,* Vol. X (Der Cicerone, II), Darmstadt, 1959, p. 78.

4 Cf. Georg W. Költzsch, "Begriff und Programm der "Brücke". In: *Künstler der Brücke. Heckel, Kirchner, Mueller, Pechstein, Schmidt-Rottluff. Gemälde, Aquarelle, Zeichnungen, Druckgraphik 1909 - 1930.* Moderne Galerie des Saarland-Museums, (Concept and Programme of the "Brücke". In Artists of the "Brücke". Heckel, Kirchner, Mueller, Pechstein, Schmidt-Rottluff. Paintings, Watercolours, Drawings, Prints, 1909 - 1930. Modern Gallery of the Museum of the Saar, Saarbrücken, 1980, 205-236.)

5 C.f. Frank Whitford, "Kirchner und das Kunsturteil." In: *Katalog Ernst Ludwig Kirchner,* ("Kirchner and art criticism") Berlin - Munich, Cologne - Zurich, 1979/80, pp. 38-45.

6 Quote from Lothar Grisebach, *E.L.Kirchners Davoser Tagebuch* (E.L. Kirchner's Davos Diary) Cologne, 1968, p. 196.

7 Paul Fechter, *Der Expressionismus,* Munich, 1914, p. 3.

8 Thus Peter Selz noted: "This book soon became almost the official guide to expressionist œsthetics ... Worringer's first essay, Abstraction and Empathy, was so important for the development of the movement itself, that Hans Tietze (in: *Lebendige Kunstwissenschaft,* Vienna, 1925, p. 25) referred to expressionism as "having characteristics which became familiar to us through Worringer's book". (Peter Selz: *German Expressionist Painting,* Berkeley and Los Angeles, 1957, pp. 8, 9).

9 Wilhelm Worringer, *Abstraktion und Einfühlung.*(Abstraction and Empathy) Quoted from the reprint, Munich, 1948, pp.16, 27, 36.

10 Dokumentarische Neuausgabe von Klaus Lankheit (New documentary edition by Klaus Lankheit). Munich, Zurich, 6th ed. 1987. This edition is used for quotations.

11 "Der Blaue Reiter" as Note 10, pp. 23, 30, 31, 35/36.

12 "Der Blaue Reiter" as Note 10, pp. 54, 55, 56.

13 "Der Blaue Reiter" as Note 10, pp. 143, 147, 154, 155.

14 "Der Blaue Reiter" as Note 10, p. 168.

15 Ludwig Coellen: *Die neue Malerei. - Der Impressionismus. Van Gogh und Cézanne. Die Romantik der neuen Malerei. Hodler. Gauguin und Matisse, Picasso und der Kubismus. Die Expressionisten* (New Painting - Impressionism. Van Gogh and Matisse, The Romanticism of new painting. Hodler. Gauguin and Matisse, Picasso and Cubism. The Expressionists), 2nd ed., Munich 1912, pp.69, 72.

16 Hans Hildebrandt, *Der Expressionismus in der Malerei. Ein Vortrag zur Einführung in das Schaffen der Gegenwart* (Expressionism in Painting. An introductory lecture on the creation of the present day). Stuttgart and Berlin, 1919, p.19.
Hildebrandt wanted to restrict the name Expressionism in the "narrower sense" to those painters who "tend towards a purely emotional, one might almost say explosive manner of creation" (id.)

17 Georg Marzynski, *Die Methode des Expressionismus . Studien zu seiner Psychologie* (The Method of Expressionism. Studies on its Psychology), Leipzig, 1920, pp.30, 51, 52.

THE ARTISTS' GROUP DIE BRÜCKE

MAGDALENA M. MOELLER

THE founding of the "Artists' Group Die Brücke" (The Bridge) in Dresden in 1905 is one of the most important events in German and international art in the twentieth century. With its imagery, its critical attitude towards traditional painting and the Academy, the movement known as Expressionism began. As well as the artistic results it produced, it manifested a new feeling about life in general, which was soon joined by poets, writers and composers.

Four architecture students formed the basis of the 'Brücke'. Fritz Bleyl and Ernst Ludwig Kirchner met in 1901, during their first semester at the Technical University in Dresden. In his *Memoirs,* Bleyl describes their meeting as follows: "One day in the first semester, I was working in the "Rohn Room" on representational geometry, doing battle with the childish exercises, when a former school friend came up to me and asked me to go down to his place at the back, because a student there, evidently an artist, had drawn all sorts of things on the edge of his Rohn sheet; this I ought to have a look at. I hurried down and was able to see the drawings around the edge, which to all appearances must have been done to fill in useless time while waiting for the professor or one of his assistants. They had been done by Ernst Ludwig Kirchner from Chemnitz, whose acquaintance I immediately sought. We became friends at once and, since we had the same goals and aspirations, a profound friendship rapidly developed. We were constantly together, either at the University, in our digs or during our evening walks in the Great Garden in Dresden. Pencil and paper were always to hand..."

Their common application to painting and drawing occupied a larger and larger part of their time and made the study of architecture retreat into the background. Being self-taught, the two friends went to work with total lack of concern and with energetic zest. Apart from the winter semester 1903/04, during which Kirchner studied at the art school run by W. Debschütz and Hermann Obrist in Munich, they had no need of any guidance from an academic course. Instead they continued their education by means of ideas they derived from the then popular magazines *Jugend* and *Simplizissimus*, which propagated the stylistic principles of *Jugendstil* (Art Nouveau). but they also followed developments in French art carefully.

"One day, Kirchner brought an illustrated volume of Meier-Gräfe on the modern French artists from some library. We were full of enthusiasm", Bleyl said later. Meier-Gräfe's "History of the Development of Modern Art" was to be a sort of guidebook not only for Bleyl and Kirchner but for the entire generation of the Expressionists.

In 1904, Bleyl and Kirchner were joined by Erich Heckel and Karl Schmidt-Rottluff . These two had met each other in a literary circle called "Vulcan" in Chemnitz (now Karl-Marx-Stadt) in 1901, while they were still at school. Apart from writing verse, they soon discovered that they shared a penchant for drawing and painting. In the summer semester of 1904, Heckel went to Dresden to study architecture. After a short time, he came to know Kirchner and Bleyl through his older brother. "It must have been around 1903, or perhaps a little later, that a new idiosyncratic personality approached our close community of friends. Unconventionally grey, dressed in an evidently specially tailored outfit and

PROFESSOR DR MAGDALENA M. MOELLER
Director of the Brücke Museum, Berlin

sporting a felt hat that had been pressed into a round shape, his high forehead, his clever, clear eyes that often lit up and shone, and his whole insistent manner led one to expect and recognize in him something significant. He could not hide the burgeoning artistry of the new." That is how Fritz Bleyl described Erich Heckel. And Kirchner, looking back, remembered: "One day a young man, loudly declaiming from *Zarathustra* and wearing neither collar nor hat came up my stairs and introduced himself as Erich Heckel."

In 1905, Karl Schmidt, who later called himself Schmidt-Rottluff after his birthplace, came to Dresden and also enrolled at the Technical University though only for two semesters. The teacher all four friends had in common, the town planner Fritz Schumacher, remembered his pupils years later: "That restlessly searching manner which every teacher of architecture knows in his students never left the "Brücke"-people: in Kirchner it rapidly acquired the character of a fairly reticent bitterness – in Heckel it was more a muted passion. It is not easy for a teacher to know to what extent he can pursue this kind of critical restlessness, since it is often combined with that purely intellectual gift which is related to an inability to create. For this reason, I was very pleased when I gradually succeeded in getting these restless elements to move along the paths of a cleanly executed true-to-nature drawing technique. But it did not last long – suddenly it stopped. I still remember the first time Heckel had started to draw a plant in the broad black-and-white manner of a woodcut,

ERICH HECKEL
Man's head –1919
Colour woodcut Cat69
Museum Folkwang, Essen

no longer paying any attention to the observation of the movements and crossing over of the leaves and instead putting onto paper something that bore a distant resemblance to the general form of the plant they were using as a model. When I was not prepared to accept the sketchy nature of the drawing, he took recourse to his right to stylize. I was of the opinion that you first had to draw accurately before you could allow yourself to stylize and referred him to some prints by William Nicholson and similar striking black-and-white artists, which I occasionally showed in order to demonstrate to the students that they were based on a close study of form. But I did not convince him. He was of the opinion that it was a matter only of the total impression, and this was how that impression was for him."

Kirchner and Bleyl completed their final architecture examinations in 1905 and now devoted themselves entirely to creative work, together with Heckel and Schmidt-Rottluff, who had both given up their studies. Their desire to be artists had become a reality. The friends enthusiastically took up Kirchner's idea of founding an artists' association. As Heckel wrote later, it was Schmidt-Rottluff who found the name: "Schmidt-Rottluff said, we could call the association 'Brücke', bridge – it was a word with many levels of meaning, it would not stand for any programme, but would in a sense lead from one shore to another. It was clear to us what we had to get away from – where we were wanting to go, however, was less clear to us." On 3rd June, 1905, the "Artists' Group Die Brücke" was founded.

Co-operative work became more intense after the founding of the group. The new creative drive, which was directed towards the representation of essentials, produced paintings with immediate form and colour. Unfettered naturalness, the liberation of Man from bourgeois constraints and the rejection of historicism emphasized the turn towards a heightened, spontaneous expression of visual language.

As painters, the friends were able to proceed much more subjectively than an architect could, and to follow their pronounced individuality entirely. Their aim was to create art as a formative event, as the result of inner sensations independently of the achievement of a particular style. The "Brücke" published its programme, which was carved in wood by Kirchner. The text consisted of a mere two sentences: "With a belief in evolution, in a new generation of creators and appreciators alike, we call upon all young people to unite in the name of Youth, with whom the future lies, let us win freedom of life and action in the face of the old establishment. We welcome all those who, with directness and sincerity, follow their creative urge." The desire for independence, of any style can be clearly heard here. It is also significant that the "Brücke" includes in its programme those who enjoy as well as those who create. In other words, passive members could join the active members. Passive members of the group – by 1910, there were 68 of these – had to pay an annual contribution of 12 Marks, later 25 Marks. For this, they received an annual portfolio of original prints.

Although the "Brücke" artists created their paintings, drawings and prints independently and with a sure instinct, they nonetheless took great interest in the Print Room of the Dresden Gallery, where there were modern prints as well as the print collection of Frederick August II, which contained works by Cranach, Dürer and Rembrandt. In the Ethnographic Museum, Kirchner discovered the carvings of the Palau Islands, and these provided a parallel close at hand to the Negro carvings to which Matisse and Picasso were devoting their attention in Paris at the same time.

In private galleries in Dresden, progressive art exhibitions were held earlier than in other German cities. In 1905, Arnold's Gallery exhibited fifty paintings by van Gogh, in 1906 over a hundred works by Belgian and French Neo-Impressionists, among them Signac, Seurat, Cross, Bernard, Denis as well as Gauguin and Valloton. In 1907 the Art Society of Saxony presented a large number of paintings by the Norwegian artist Edvard Munch, which had a profound effect on Kirchner in particular. In 1907, there was also the opportunity of seeing works by the Impressionists Claude Monet, Alfred Sisley and Camille Pissarro. There was another large van Gogh exhibition in 1908, when Richter's Art Salon showed a retrospective of a hundred paintings. The Fauves also held an exhibition there in the same year. The works of van Dongen, Vlaminck, Guérin and Friesz had just as free an approach to artistic materials as the works of the "Brücke" members. They also employed spontaneous drawing and a glowing language of colours in a new way.

The stylistic development of the "Brücke" from beginnings in the manner of *Jugendstil* (Art Nouveau), through a pointillistic style of expression oriented to Neo-Impressionism and van Gogh, to their own style – that of 'Brücke'-Expressionism, – was completed in 1908/09.

Far-reaching changes had taken place in the painters' thinking about their pictures. Starting out from forms of nature, figures and objects were simplified more and more without, however, stylizing them or loading symbols onto their content. The artists tried to crystallize an expressive element from nature, and in the process, distortion became a stylistic hallmark as the result of a quite subjective, ecstatic sensation. Simplified, concise lines, broad-surface composition and clear glowing colours are the characteristics of the new style reflecting the physical restlessness of the artists and their heightened desire to create. In their struggle for a new art, the painters had grown so alike that something had emerged which might be described as a community style.

Kirchner can probably be said to be the most versatile, most excited and most expressive member of the group; his pictures possess a spirituality that makes them superior to the works of other "Brücke" artists. Schmidt-Rottluff had a powerful temperament, which, though less sensitive, was able to evoke a monumental pictorial expression from a simplified model in nature. Heckel is regarded as the lyrical talent of the group. In his paintings, a creative-eruptive manner is tempered and governed by a less emotional and more poetic desire for form. The aggressive element is absent in his expression. In the case of Pechstein, the "Brücke"-style is expressed in strong colours with a decorative note.

Apart from painting, the woodcut became the predominant means of expression for the "Brücke" artists. With Kirchner, Schmidt-Rottluff and Heckel, it became a medium for strict and concise formulation of images. Kirchner wrote about the significance of prints for the "Brücke" : "The will that drives an artist to do graphic work is perhaps partly the endeavour to mould the unique loose form of the drawing firmly and definitively. The technical manipulations, on the other hand, liberate forces in the artist which are not shown to advantage in the far easier manual operations involved in drawing or painting. The mechanical process of printing creates a unity from the different phases of the work. The formative process can be extended as long as desired without any danger. There is a great thrill in attaining the ultimate in expression and perfection of form by revising the work again and again for weeks or even months without the plate losing its freshness. The secret thrill which surrounded the invention of printing in the Middle Ages is still felt today by anyone who occupies himself seriously with printing and all the details of its craft.." After Albrecht Dürer, this long-neglected, almost forgotten technique was taken up anew and taken to new artistic peaks. The woodcuts of the "Brücke" form an essential part of German art history.

The "Artists' Group Die Brücke", consisting of the four architecture students expanded by several members soon after its foundation. In January 1906, Emil Nolde had an exhibition in the Arnold Gallery in Dresden. His unorthodox paintings aroused a lively interest among the "Brücke" group, with the result that Schmidt-Rottluff wrote the following letter to Nolde on 4th February: "I'll come to the point straight away – the local artists' group "Brücke" would consider it an honour to welcome you as a member. Of course, you probably know as little about the "Brücke" as we did about you before your exhibition at Arnold's. Well, one of the aims of the "Brücke" is to gather around it all revolutionary and fermenting ele-

ments – that is what the name "Brücke" means. Apart from this, the group also organizes several exhibitions a year to tour Germany, so that the individual artist is relieved of the business side. A further goal is the creation of our own exhibition space – as yet an ideal, since we lack the money. Now, dear Mr Nolde, think how and what you like, with this letter we have tried to pay our debt for your colour storms. Yours in devotion and homage, the Artists' Group Die Brücke."

Nolde became a member of the group for eighteen months but then left as a result of personal differences with other members. In his biography, he says: "It was difficult for me to tolerate the perhaps inevitable friction in both personal and artistic respects, and I did not like the uniformity that was developing in the young artists, who were often extremely similar in their works. I then continued on my artist's way alone again. But I remained well disposed to them in my attitudes and their friend in artistic matters." Nolde benefited from his brief membership in so far as he adopted the woodcut, which was to play a large role in his work. The "Brücke" artists, for their part, learned from him the techniques of etching.

In 1906, Max Pechstein also joined the group. Heckel had met him in the spring at the "Third German Exhibition of Arts and Crafts" held in Dresden from 12 May to 31 October, where Pechstein was executing paintings for the interior decoration. Heckel had continued to work as an assistant to the architect Wilhelm Kreis until 1907 and was also involved in preparations for the exhibition. After an apprenticeship as an interior decorator, Pechstein had gone to the Dresden School of Arts and Crafts from 1900 to 1902 and concluded his training at the Dresden Academy of Art as a student in a master class from 1902 to 1906. In addition, he was awarded the State Prize of Saxony, called the "Rome Prize", which gave him a certain lead over the other "Brücke" artists who were self-taught and as yet unknown.

Also in 1906, the Swiss painter Cuno Amiet was won over to the "Brücke" group. After they had seen his works in Arnold's Gallery, Heckel wrote to him on 1 September, 1906: "Honoured Sir, it was with admiration and enthusiasm that we saw your works and we take the liberty of inviting you to join our group, called "Brücke". We unanimously recognized you as one of us and hope that you will support our cause in striving towards the same artistic goals. Our group would be extraordinarily pleased to have found in you a comrade in arms and champion for its cause." Amiet accepted the invitation without hesitation. Later, the group was joined by the Dutchman Kees van Dongen, whom Pechstein had met in Paris in 1908, Axel Gallén-Kallela from Finland and Lambertus Zijl from Holland. Through this growth, the group acquired an international complexion. Edvard Munch, however, did not accept the invitation to join. Approaches to Henri Matisse also remained unsuccessful. The Hamburg painter Franz Nölken became a member for a short time, but he ultimately left for Paris to join the Matisse school. Otto Mueller joined the "Brücke" in 1910 and was closely associated with its affairs. Finally, the last artist to join the group was the Prague artist Bohumil Kubista, although the contact was not intensive. In 1909, Bleyl, who had been a foundation member, left the group in order to devote himself fully to architecture.

By organizing exhibitions, the group found a strategy for presenting its new kind of work to the public and gaining recognition. The group's first exhibition of paintings, water colours and drawings took place in the showroom of the K.F.M. Seifert lamp factory in the Dresden suburb of Löbtau in the autumn of 1906. Contact with this firm had been made by Heckel, who was the manager of the group due to his talent for organization. Karl-Max Seifert gave his permission for the exhibition and at the same time became a passive member of the group. In his salesroom, where lamps hung from the ceiling, the cloth-covered walls were hung with pictures. A second exhibition, consisting only of prints, also took place here in the winter of 1906/07. There were very few visitors, and the press took no notice of this exhibition of unknown artists in an out of the way venue.

It was in 1907 that the "Brücke" finally made the leap into the leading galleries of Dresden. The exhibition in Richter's Art Salon created a stir, as did the 1910 exhibition in Arnold's Gallery, which is now considered one of the pioneering exhibitions of the twentieth century. In addition, the "Brücke" sent travelling exhibitions throughout Germany, to Switzerland and even to Scandinavia. More than thirty exhibitions had been organized by 1910

and the group participated in numerous other mixed exhibitions. Through participation in the "International Exhibition of the Special Association of West German Friends of Art and Artists" in Cologne in 1912, the "Brücke" attained the peak of its popularity.

Other exhibitions of decisive importance for the group were held by the "New Secession" in Berlin. After Pechstein had successfully exhibited in the 1909 "Berlin Secession", run by Max Liebermann, they exhibited there as a group in 1910. But the Secession had become increasingly traditional and was disturbed by the increased representation of the young avant-garde whose works it considered as an affront to its own. The rejected artists – who apart from the "Brücke", included Nolde and Christian Rohlfs – thereupon founded the "New Secession" under the direction of Max Pechstein.

Kirchner, Schmidt-Rottluff and Heckel moved to Berlin in 1911. Pechstein had been living there since 1908 and had made many contacts for the group, so the move to the capital appeared attractive. As in Dresden, the artists rented studios close to one another, but despite regular mutual visits, personal division set in. The Berlin phase of the "Brücke" marks the gradual dissolution of the group. The all-powerful, hectic and aggressive metropolis contributed to their alienation, for each of the "Brücke" artists reacted differently to the new surroundings. 1911 witnessed the change from a collective style to many individual ones. In the street scenes by Kirchner, the soft Dresden style hardened and changed to sharp forms with acute angles.

Influences of cubism found their way into Kirchner's art and became a means of expressing the hectic and aggressive elements of the metropolis. The flow of his brush-strokes in the Berlin years has an unnatural, vibrating, nervosity; his colours lose their glow and become – not least as a result of the use of distemper to which Otto Mueller introduced him – gloomy and despairing. In the second "Brücke" style, which heightens Expressionism to an extreme degree, the nature previously dominant becomes anti-nature. The artificiality of big-city life is symbolized by the reduction of given reality to hieroglyphics of expression. In the case of Schmidt-Rottluff too, allusions to a cubist language can be observed, as well as an increased orientation towards Negro art. Block-like compositional elements displace the powerful, free brush-strokes of the years before. In contrast to Kirchner, he did not turn to depicting the metropolis, but continued to paint landscapes as before, deriving from his sojourns in Dangast regularly every summer from 1907 and from his particular love of nature. Heckel began to join the striving for an ordering architecture in his paintings by working towards a style dominated by jagged lines and small formal elements complete in themselves. The translation of the natural impression into a formal unity was the primary problem of his Berlin period. Otto Mueller's pictures create the effect of being variations on a single theme in the centre of which man stands in nature. He did not work out his visual language until 1910, that is, after he became a member of the "Brücke". Absolute harmony of art and life are perfectly realized here. Back to nature, characteristic for the "Brücke" in its first phase, became a primal experience for Mueller. He saw the human being as a quintessential part of nature. His figures are peaceful, (without expressive pathos), virtually symbols of the hope for an earthly paradise.

The members tried to counter the disintegration of the group that was becoming apparent by making the decision to leave the "New Secession" together. Pechstein, who alone refused, was excluded from the "Brücke" as a result in 1912.

Apart from this, in an attempt to re-define the common aspects of the group, it was decided to produce a "Chronicle of the Brücke Artists' Group". If the group had already been threatened by the exclusion of Pechstein, it was, curiously enough, the Chronicle that was to lead to the dissolution of the group. The others felt hurt by the high-handed way Kirchner presented them. Heckel later declared: "We planned the production of a chronicle for 1913, which was to contain hand-made prints and photos of paintings by all of us (these latter taken by Kirchner). Kirchner wrote the accompanying text. This text did not match the view Schmidt-Rottluff, Otto Mueller or I had of the facts, nor our anti-programme approach, so that we decided not to produce the Chronicle. Each member received his prints and his part of the text. Kirchner later did cut the title page with the four portraits in Switzerland and assembled a few copies."

In May 1913, the passive members of the "Brücke" were informed of its dissolution. The Chronicle was only an external cause for the break, which really had occurred long before, ever since the move to Berlin. What the "Brücke" had set as its goal in 1905, – the creation of a new art – had been attained. On the basis of what had been achieved together, the individual members were now able to develop freely and unfold their own styles without hindrance.

THE BLUE RIDER
& ITS BEGINNINGS

ARMIN ZWEITE

THE "Blue Rider" and Munich are synonymous. The Bavarian capital played a decisive role for a short moment on the eve of World War I when, in a radical change, the bases of modern art were formulated and, unnoticed by a broader public, the avant-garde found its way there. The emigré artists in Munich were crucially important: Wassily Kandinsky from Moscow, Marianne von Werefkin and Alexei von Jawlensky from St Petersburg, Paul Klee from Berne, August Macke from Bonn and Gabriele Münter from Westphalia. Only Franz Marc came from Munich. The city's power to attract this constellation becomes clear when we consider what it had to offer at the end of the nineteenth century.

Since the achievement of Ludwig I, who wanted to create an "Athens on the Isar" during his regency (1825-48), and particularly after the great international exhibition of 1869, Munich was regarded as a vital centre of the visual arts. Without attempting a comprehensive account of the cultural climate at the turn of the century, a few points suffice to indicate the state of the arts at that time. Literature and art were marked very distinctly by a rejection of Naturalism. Neo-Idealism and a particular variety of Symbolism dominated the scene, and painters like Arnold Böcklin and Franz von Stuck had their greatest triumphs here in the 1890s. The first "Secession" in the German-language region split from the Artists' Association in Munich in 1892, to hold exhibitions free of any jury, thus giving renewed importance to the criterion of quality. A little later, from 1896 onwards, two very influential magazines appeared in

Munich: *Simplizissimus*, a satirical journal, and *Jugend* (Youth) which gave its name to the style of a whole epoch. For many years the city was a centre of *Jugendstil* (Art Nouveau) in which the arts and crafts predominated. Despite its conservative character, Munich's great museums, important Academy, private galleries, exhibition rooms, publishers, theatres, orchestras and international bohemians provided an infrastructure that was at least partly serviceable in promoting new artistic ideas, without plunging the new elements into instant competition with other avant-garde tendencies – as was the case in Paris, for instance.

Many of the artists considered here may appear romantic and far removed from everyday life. However idealistic in intent, some of them certainly proved to be pragmatists in realising their aims. Kandinsky very rapidly grasped the social mechanisms at the basis of the art agencies and the marketing of art. He was aware from the beginning that propaganda and publicising the intentions of works of art were just as important as the presentation itself. Thus it is not surprising that the "Blue Rider" exhibition mounted in the Thannhauser Gallery around New Year 1911/12, an exhibition which had come about more by accident than by design, was organised by the editors of the "Blue Rider". Those same editors were busy preparing to print one of the most significant manifestoes of the twentieth century, *The Blue Rider Almanac*.

Before we return to this topic, first a few notes on the most important and influential figures of the Munich avant-garde. Wassily Kandinsky, born 1866 in Moscow, had completed courses in economics, law and ethnography when he decided in 1896 to become an artist. In Munich he took

DR ARMIN ZWEITE
Director of the Lenbach House Municipal Gallery, Munich

some lessons in art, but was basically self taught. He painted small landscapes in the impressionist manner and, as early as 1901, became president of the artists' association "Phalanx", which only lasted until 1904. As an art teacher he came to know Gabriele Münter, who attended the "Phalanx" school because women were not admitted to art studies at the Academy. Münter became his constant companion, and together they made numerous trips through Europe from 1904 onwards. Their stay of some twelve months in Paris in 1906/07 was of particular significance, for Kandinsky evidently became acquainted with the works of the Fauves at that time. The liberation of colour as pure expressive value which the Fauves instigated had such a profound influence on Kandinsky that he turned away from his romantically historicising subjects to try out the new pictorial idioms in landscapes.

Jawlensky too was stimulated by contemporary French painting in a decisive way. He met Henri Matisse in Paris, but of greater significance was his friendship with the Benedictine priest and painting monk Willibrord Verkade, with whom he shared a studio for some time in 1907. As a Gauguin pupil, Verkade reinforced Jawlensky in his endeavours to simplify the compositional structure of his works and to emphasise forms by dark outlining. This decisive change in his work indicated how the painter had recourse to Gauguin's cloisonnism. He also assimilated the powerful impetus of van Gogh, one of whose landscape paintings Jawlensky bought at a Munich exhibition at the beginning of 1908. He tried to synthesise both these influences with orna-

Gabriele Münter 1905

mental colour figuration in the same way as Matisse.

Werefkin and Jawlensky, Münter and Kandinsky were acquainted from earlier meetings, but did not reach a fruitful rapport until all four met to paint together in the summer of 1908 in Murnau, a small market town some 60 km south of Munich. In retrospect, Gabriele Münter wrote of this working holiday: "After a short period of agony, I made a great leap there – from nature depiction – more or less impressionistic – to feeling the content, to abstraction – to giving the essence. It was a beautiful, interesting, joyous time of work with many discussions about art. I particularly liked showing my work to Jawlensky – on the one hand he liked praising things and did so at length but on the other, he also explained things to me – gave me some of what he had experienced and gained and spoke of a "synthesis". We all worked hard. Kandinsky has undergone a wonderful development since then."

While Werefkin remained faithful to her basically Symbolist position, Kandinsky and Münter oriented themselves towards Jawlensky, who occupied the most progressive position in the summer of 1908. However, under the impression of the paintings he had seen in Paris, Kandinsky soon began to imbue the objective reference points in his impressive landscapes with an element of mystery. In his paintings of this period expressive gestures are paired with colouring that is largely emancipated from the real appearance of the objects represented. Kandinsky rapidly went beyond Jawlensky's intentions. The latter's slogan of "synthesis" probably meant simplicity in the first instance. In contrast, Kandinsky's paintings make it clear that the merging of different motif areas and the transformation of spatial relationships into flat correspondences was an important step on the way towards the distortion of depicted reality and towards the dissolution of its phenomenal forms. Kandinsky's Murnau landscapes are a decisive pre-condition of abstraction, while Jawlensky's works from the same period, from 1908 or 1909 onwards, constitute an even stricter stylisation of figuration.

Their work together in the Bavarian high country lasted for a relatively short time. The paintings of Jawlensky, Kandinsky and Münter wrestled with essentially the same problem. At the beginning of their artistic dialogue, it was Jawlensky who set the crucial directions, and these had an extraordinarily liberating effect especially on Gabriele Münter, no doubt also encouraging Kandinsky to set off on a path that soon had him aiming for quite different goals from his Russian compatriot's. The discourse of the modern movement, reflected here in the avant-garde tendencies the artists had assimilated, reveals an additional, completely different component – one which assumed a considerable significance especially for Kandinsky. It was evidently Gabriele Münter who drew the attention of her friends and colleagues to Bavarian folk art and stimulated a fruitful discussion on this subject. While Jawlensky took scant interest in it and Werefkin made a few excursions in this direction, for Kandinsky it opened up an entirely new terrain which had far-reaching consequences for the formal and iconographic aspects of his art. This was peasant *verre eglomisé,* and its naïve spontaneity struck Kandinsky and Münter as manifestations of an unselfconscious desire for expression. They collected pictures of religious subjects,

Wassily Kandinsky
All Saints' Day I – 1911
Glass painting
Städtische Galerie im Lenbachhaus, Munich

copied them and transmitted the stimulus into their own work.

Their interest in folk art should, however, be seen against the background of avant-garde art in Europe generally. In their search for spontaneous expression, painters and sculptors around the turn of the century discovered the cultures outside Europe, the art of naïve people, of children and the mentally disturbed. As is well known, the cubists were inspired by African masks and sculptures. The members of the "Brücke" directed their attention to the cult objects of Polynesia. Following the contemporary trend, Jawlensky owned numerous Japanese wood cuts. At about this same time, Münter and Kandinsky began a collection of children's drawings, which is intact to this day. The repertoire of forms they observed in such varied endeavours, which were surprising on account of their strangeness, seemed to the painters in Paris, Dresden or Munich, to be suited to destroying the outmoded traditions of the Academies and to replacing them with fresh, unspent artistic principles. The particular goals pursued by Kandinsky can be deduced from his work and activities until 1914. His attempt to orient his own life at least temporarily to the life of the village people, illusory though it was bound to be, led him to wear Bavarian folk costume when he was in Murnau and to paint the simple furniture for the house Münter had bought at the edge of the township in bright colours. All this corresponded to the desire to set new, pioneering directions in the cultural life of the metropolis Munich.

It is highly possible, though it cannot be proved, that their stay in Murnau gave them the idea of showing the results of their work in public and endeavouring to spread their insights. Since the large exhibiting institutions were closed to avant-garde artists, and the private galleries did not want to become involved with the new directions, the option that remained was to organise themselves. Who ultimately took the initiative to give their intentions more weight by banding together with other painters with similar views is not known. No doubt the memory of the secessionist movements, which succeeded in promoting new ideas against established ones, was an important precedent for all of them, but particularly for Jawlensky. It was he who was initially the figurehead of the "New Artists' Group of Munich" founded in January 1909. Alexander Kanoldt, Adolf Erbslöh, Paul Baum, Vladimir Bechtejeff, Pierre Girieud, Erma Bossi and several others belonged to this group, which was dominated by Russian artists. They were the ones who wrote the founding statement, which says among other things: "We are proceeding from the assumption that, apart from the impressions the artist receives from the external world, from nature, he also continually collects experiences in an inner world. The search for artistic forms which will express the mutual interpenetration of all these experiences, – for forms which must be liberated from everything incidental, in order to express more forcefully the essential, – in short, the striving for an artistic synthesis...this seems to us the motto uniting more and more artists at present..."

The first exhibition of the New Artists' Group of Munich took place in December 1909 in the Thannhauser Modern Gallery in Munich, and a second one at the same venue in September

Wassily Kandinsky
Painted wooden furniture – 1910

Wassily Kandinsky
Poster for New Artists' Group – 1909

1910. This second show was of particular significance, for a number of international painters and sculptors had been invited to participate, Braque, Derain, van Dongen, Picasso, Vlaminck and Rouault among them. In the catalogue accompanying the exhibition, Kandinsky published an essay which is informative in so far as it clearly documents the distance between them and the other Munich painters. The contrast between an objective impression of nature and a subjective feeling which, as Jawlensky saw it, was synthesised in the production of the painting, was extended by Kandinsky into a collision of the spiritual with the material. For him, painting becomes the "saying of the secret through the secret". With such terminology, Kandinsky departed from the common ground on which he and Jawlensky had been able to communicate during their work together in Murnau. Ultimately, it was the Symbolist undercurrent of Kandinsky's thought which gained the upper hand and began to alienate him from most of the other members of the group. Erbslöh and Kanoldt appear to have become increasingly sceptical of him after mimetic motifs began to vanish more and more from his paintings.

The second exhibition of the New Artists' Group of Munich travelled to Karlsruhe, Mannheim, Hagen, Berlin and Dresden. It marked the high point of the Group's activities and also initiated its demise. The exhibition was criticized vehemently, but there was also enthusiastic approval. Franz Marc wrote an enthusiastic review, in which he said: "The completely spiritualised and dematerialised inwardness of feeling is a problem in painting which our fathers, the artists of the nineteenth century, never so much as attempted to tackle. This bold attempt to spiritualise the material reality to which Impressionism clings with such dogged obstinancy is a necessary reaction which began with Gauguin in Pont-Aven and has already given rise to innumerable experiments. The reason why this latest experiment by the New Artists' Group seems to us so promising is that, in addition to their highly spiritualised meaning, the pictures of the group offer highly valuable examples of rhythm, composition, and colour theory."

"The completely spiritualised and dematerialised inwardness of feeling" – this is the crucial slogan to which Marc felt bound and so it was inevitable that he should seek close contact with these painters who, in his opinion, were able to realise this notion in very diverse ways. The second exhibition of the New Artists' Group of Munich may have had a liberating effect on him, since he thought he perceived in it an endorsement of his own endeavours.

Franz Marc was born in Munich in 1880 the son of the painter Wilhelm Marc. He was uncertain whether he should become a theologian or an artist, eventually deciding in favour of painting and had enrolled at the Munich Academy to study under Gabriel Hackl and Wilhelm von Dietz. He received a traditional training, so his early work adheres to a moderately modern style without any high points worth mentioning. However, his past achievements came more and more into doubt as a result of the impressions made by several trips to Paris, for he was unable

Maria & Franz Marc 1911

August Macke 1903

to follow any one model definitely. Marc had already begun to circle around the thematic centre of his oeuvre during this phase. What particularly concerned him were representations of animals. For him the creatures became symbols of natural innocence and pure, unspoilt life.

While Marc knew a lot of artists in Munich, he could not find any productive exchange on artistic matters. This changed suddenly in 1910, when he met August Macke. An intense relationship developed. Macke had studied at the Düsseldorf Academy in 1904/05, but, stimulated by several trips to Paris, leaned strongly towards French art. In 1909/10, he was living at Lake Tegern near Munich, whence his meeting with Marc came about. This meeting was important to Marc because the Berlin collector, Bernhard Koehler, a relative of Macke, bought two of Marc's paintings on Macke's advice.

When Marc began his association with the New Artists' Group of Munich, he found Kandinsky an inspiring conversationalist. Kandinsky, for his part, felt misunderstood by some of the members of the group, with the result that the first disagreements within the group took place in the spring and summer of 1911. Marc anticipated the conflicts. There was a row during the Group's jury session of 1 and 2 December 1911, when Kandinsky's "Composition V" was not voted in. While Jawlensky and Werefkin remained members of the New Artists' Group of Munich, Kandinsky, Marc and Münter left in protest.

There was nothing unusual in the fact that new secessions arose out of old ones, groups split, or artistic movements fell apart in the late nineteenth and early twentieth century. Werefkin and Jawlensky already had experienced this in St Petersburg, even if they were only spectators. However, what made the conflict in the New Artists' Group of Munich significant was its critical time in the historical process. The birth of abstract art is linked with the name of Kandinsky. The origins of the crisis can probably be attributed to this fact. It is conceivable that Jawlensky and Werefkin, despite their sympathy for their compatriot, did not share his goals and, in this instance, distanced themselves from him. It is also possible that the other artists regarded Kandinsky's development as being on the wrong track: the intellectual basis of their art centred upon the notion of "synthesis" and excluded the total elimination of representation. Kandinsky had by no means completed this transformation by 1911, but he had turned away from naturalistic motifs to the extent that his paintings were found baffling, particularly his main works such as the violently controversial *Composition V,* which bore no resemblance to the landscape studies of his Murnau phase. Ultimately, the cosmological aspect of Kandinsky's and Marc's aims, their aspiration to transcend reality, made them more or less incomprehensible to the others.

Soon after the break, Marc and Kandinsky organised the first "Blue Rider" exhibition, which took place in the rooms of the Thannhauser Gallery at the same time as the third exhibition of the New Artists' Group of Munich. Fourteen artists were represented: Henri Rousseau, Albert Bloch, David and Vladimir Burljuk, Heinrich Campendonk, Robert Delaunay, Elisabeth Epstein, Eugen Kahler, Wassily Kandinsky, August Macke, Franz Marc, Gabriele Münter, Jean Bloé Niestlé and Arnold Schönberg.

The first Blue Rider Exhibition in December 1911 near Thannhausen

This was no doubt a very heterogeneous selection, but Kandinsky and Marc attempted to justify the absence of a unifying concept in the catalogue: "In this small exhibition, we are not attempting to put forward a single precise and special form, rather our aim is to show in the very differences of the forms represented, how the inner desire of the artists manifests itself in various ways." The exhibition was well documented by photographs. What it highlighted was the contrast between "great abstraction" exemplified by the works of Marc, Delaunay and Kandinsky, and "great realism" presented in the first instance by the paintings of "Le Douanier" Henri Rousseau and the composer Arnold Schönberg, but also by the superficially naïve pictures of Jean Bloé Niestlé. In the exhibition at Thannhauser the contrast, which concerned Kandinsky again and again in his theoretical writings, could not be shown very clearly, as the large format works of Marc, Delaunay and Kandinsky predominated and the other side made little visual impact. The discrepancy was so blatant, Niestlé withdrew his work from the exhibition before it finished and Schönberg was also hesitant to participate in further stages of the project once he had been invited to show in a mixed exhibition in Budapest.

A second exhibition followed in February 1912, this time at the art dealer Hans Goltz's gallery. It contained over 300 watercolours, drawings, wood-cuts, etchings, etc. This time importance was given to international participation and representing the other significant German avant-garde movement which called itself the "Brücke". Erich Heckel, Ernst Ludwig Kirchner, Otto Mueller, Emil Nolde and Max Pechstein were well represented with works which formed a vivid contrast to those of Georges Braque, Pablo Picasso, Maurice Vlaminck, Natalia Goncharova, Mikhail Larionov, Kasimir Malevich and others. In addition, a group of Russian folk prints from Kandinsky's collection were incorporated; Kandinsky attached great importance to these traditional, popular pictures as examples of "great realism". In contrast to the earlier exhibition of paintings, which travelled to many cities, there were no other venues for this project.

Despite the lack of balance of the first exhibition, which must be attributed at least in part to hasty preparation, it should be stressed that the "Blue Rider" was ultimately the personal achievement of two kindred personalities. Marc and Kandinsky were able to express their ideas much more forcefully in the famous *Blue Rider Almanac,* as they had more time to plan the publication than they had for the two exhibitions at the Thannhauser and Goltz galleries. Moreover, the first exhibition had been designed to put the works of the "New Artists' Group", shown in adjoining rooms at Thannhauser, into the shade.

Ever since the summer of 1911, when the conflicts within the "New Artists' Group" worsened, Kandinsky had plans for an almanac, and he advised Marc about it on 19.6.1911. This letter is practically the birth certificate of the "Blue Rider". Naturally, the project could not be realised at once, and the volume did not appear until the middle of May 1912, some time after the epoch-making exhibitions. Kandinsky described the way the title was found in the "Kunstblatt" of 1930. "We made up the name 'Blue Rider' over coffee in the leafy garden at Sindelsdorf. Both of us loved blue, Marc – horses, I – riders." Horses and riders played an important role in Kandinsky's romantic paint-

Wassily Kandinsky
Cover for *The Blue Rider Almanac*

ings, where they are symbols of longing and of departure. Blue was for him a "typical heavenly colour" that beckons humans to infinity and awakens their longing for purity and a world beyond the senses. It is also possible that the name alludes to the "blue flower" of German Romanticism. As his painting "Blue Horses" shows, Marc was thinking along similar lines, hence the "Blue Rider" symbolised a turning point in art. Kandinsky expressed this endeavour on the title page of the *Almanac*. The rider is very closely linked to Kandinsky's manifold ideas for paintings and is clearly reminiscent of the figure of Saint George.

The exhibitions and book belong together. The fundamental significance of the exhibitions and programmatic text lies in the inclusion not only of avant-garde works, but also of examples of Egyptian and East Asian art, folk art, paintings by children and lay people. Their goal was a synthesis of the most varied genres, directions and epochs. Franz Marc, for instance, summarised their common striving as follows: "In their world view, both (Cézanne and El Greco) felt the mystical-inward construction which is the great problem facing today's generation." Kandinsky came to the conclusion that "The external effect (of a work of art) can be different from the internal effect, which is produced by the inner sound, which is one of the most powerful and profound means of expression in every composition." In another place, the principle underlying the selection of the paintings in the *Almanac*: "...of prime importance in the question of form is whether or not form has arisen out of internal necessity." This concept of internal necessity plays a large role in the considerations of the artists, and we find it occurs in a similar guise in Klee's work.

There are no fewer than three contributions by Franz Marc in the *Almanac*. "The spirit breaks down fortresses" – with these words he ends his programmatic introductory essay titled *Spiritual Treasures*. The motto seems to summarise the world of the imagination and horizons of thought of this important artist who became more popular than any other German painter, with the possible exception of August Macke.

The "great spiritual" which Kandinsky, the intellectual among the avant-garde, had conjured up in Munich, became a touchstone for Marc as well. He tried to abstract his pictorial formulations from the concrete forms of reality and to reach a symbolic expression. Cleansing and purifying from the slag of worldliness became stock phrases of his thought and the figurative and landscape motifs of his earlier work were replaced almost without exception by representations of animals. In this guise the painter believed he could embed living creation in the cosmos, as he imagined it, by means of a drastically simplified language of forms and specific colour symbolism. In a world deprived of gods, he was concerned to "create for our time symbols that belong on the altars of future spiritual religions and behind which their technical procreator disappears".

In a phase of increasing mechanization of life, the dissolution of all social ties and value standards, and under the pressure of the industrialisation of Wilhelminian Germany, his notions of the binding force and general applicability of a new

art certainly had the power to fascinate. A radical rejection of contemporary art practices, of a worn out formal repertoire and obsolete subjects was a necessary consequence of the path Marc and Kandinsky had chosen. "The longing for indivisible being", Marc noted around 1912/13, "liberation from the deception of our senses of our ephemeral life is the ground note of all art". It was evident that he wanted to break with naturalism and impressionism and to take the step from the representational image to the Idea. In the background was also the conviction, a binding one for Kandinsky, that spiritual values had to replace material ones.

Reading Macke's essay in the *Almanac*, one sees that this painter also asked himself the question whether and in what way pictorial form is "an expression of mysterious forces". The purpose of art was not to reflect reality or to be a merely formal exercise, but should again become a fetish, as it were, a crystallisation of spiritual, indeed mystical forces. Thus, at this stage, Macke and Marc developed in a similar direction to Münter's and Kandinsky's, but with the crucial difference that the Russian painter cut the ropes with tradition even more decisively, and at the same time was searching for a theoretical justification for doing so.

In this regard, it should be noted that Kandinsky's essay *On the Spiritual in Art* appeared at the end of 1911. In this book he emphasised the liberation of painting from naturalist-objective content and demanded that the artist turn to the idea of a free, universal spiritual body of themes and a set of forms and colours appropriate to it. The emphatic antimaterialism and the propagation of the purely spiritual as the only goal worth striving

Wassily Kandinsky
Cover for *On the Spiritual in Art*

for, make much of the content of his thesis resemble the irrationalism common at the turn of the century, and in this, the parallels with Theosophy are particularly apparent. There is no doubt that Kandinsky was sympathetic to many of Rudolf Steiner's ideas, but it would be an exaggeration to assume he was an uncritical follower of that topical doctrine.

Looking at Kandinsky's paintings and graphics from this transitional period, concrete objects such as riders, castles, mountains, trees, boats, etc, are still discernible. The artist has spoken at length about the problem occurring in his work, namely the connection of representational motifs with abstract elements. Between representation and total abstraction "lie the infinite number of forms in which both elements are present, and where either the material or the abstract predominates. These forms are at present the store from which the artist borrows all the individual elements of his creations. Today, the artist cannot manage exclusively with purely abstract forms. These forms are imprecise for him. To limit oneself exclusively to the imprecise is to deprive oneself of possibilities, to exclude the purely human and thus impoverish one's means of expression." In these sentences Kandinsky exactly described the scope of his painting of the pre-war years.

It extended from purely abstract compositions to works which retained a narrative core. It seems especially important to stress that the creation of paintings without reference to objective motifs was not the outcome of a purely formal process

Wassily Kandinsky 1913

of reduction, but resulted from a long endeavour to comprehend something purely spiritual and psychic in a *Klang* liberated from all material encumbrance.

This epoch-making achievement broke with the traditional European concept of a picture. For Kandinsky it was linked with the hope that a spiritual cosmos would emerge. It was in art – according to him – that the spiritual turning point first became perceptible. Literature, music and art, in his view, were "the first and most sensitive realms where this spiritual change becomes noticeable in real form. These spheres immediately reflect the murky present; they provide an intimation of that greatness which first becomes noticeable only to a few, just a tiny point, and which for the masses does not exist at all." In Kandinsky's theoretical conception, a romantic utopia was combined with an avowedly anti-materialistic and anti-scientific stance – these two last aspects inherited from Symbolism, and beyond that, pointing back to German Romanticism.

In retrospect, it should be noted that the two exhibitions at the Thannhauser and Goltz Galleries and the *The Blue Rider Almanac* made Munich a true centre of the European avant-garde for a brief period. The prerequisite for the exhibitions and publication to become a reality was the visionary involvement of Kandinsky and his co-operation with Franz Marc. While the latter put his efforts into turning their ideas into practical reality, it seems the decisive spiritual impulses came from

Kandinsky. Without wishing to lessen the contributions of the other protagonists, it has to be stressed that the Russian painter was the first to set the new directions and was prepared to take the biggest risks in both conceptual and aesthetic respects. Hence it is significant that Hugo Ball saw in him a "prophet of the rebirth".

We saw above that the name "Blue Rider" is linked to a very few events: two exhibitions in the Thannhauser and Goltz Galleries at the end of 1911 and the beginning of 1912, and the production of the *Almanac* by Wassily Kandinsky and Franz Marc. A broadly-based artistic movement did not result from these manifestations, even though the exhibition of paintings was shown – with some changes in its composition – in many European cities: Cologne, Berlin, Frankfurt, Hamburg, Rotterdam, Amsterdam, Vienna, Prague, Budapest, Oslo, Stockholm and Gothenburg, to name only the most important. The ideas were spread through the circulation of the paintings and the distribution of the *Almanac*, which appeared in a slightly modified second edition in the early summer of 1914.

Kandinsky's book *On the Spiritual in Art* also proved to be extremely important.

By the outbreak of World War I, at the very latest, the movement was spent. Differences of opinion had arisen between individuals earlier, and plans to edit a second volume of the *Almanac* could not be realised. August Macke and Franz Marc died on the battlefields of France; Werefkin, Jawlensky and Kandinsky as Russian citizens were obliged to leave Germany. Only Paul Klee continued his stay in Munich, interrupted by his military service, but by summer 1914 he became one of the founding members of the "New Munich Secession", a moderate association of artists who did not take up the central ideas of Marc and Kandinsky. In October 1920 Klee was offered a position at the Bauhaus and a year later moved to Weimar. By that time, Munich had lapsed from its rôle as a centre of the avant-garde. Kandinsky later nostalgically recalled the time before 1914. The impulses of the "Blue Rider", it seemed to him, had not fallen on fruitful ground in the city of origin, and Munich had sunk into self-satisfaction and provinciality. In 1930 he wrote: "Today – after so many years – the spiritual atmo-sphere of beautiful Munich, a city that despite everything remains dear to me, has altered fundamentally. Schwabing, in those days so loud and bustling, has become silent – not a sound can be heard from there. A pity for Munich, and even more of a pity for funny, somewhat eccentric and self-confident Schwabing, in whose streets a person – be it man or woman – not carrying a palette, a canvas, or at the very least a portfolio was immediately conspicuous. Like an 'intruder' in a 'nest'. Everybody painted ... or wrote poetry, or played music, or learned to dance. In every house one could find under the eaves at least two studios, in many of which not so much painting went on as constant discussion, debate, philosophising, and a good measure of drinking (which depended less upon one's moral state than upon one's pocket)."

The "Brücke" and the "Blue Rider" were the two pivotal German artistic movements dedicated to modernism in Wilhelminian Germany. The fact that the painters in Dresden and Munich turned to an aesthetic of the immediate, the essential and the elementary culminated in paintings which were conspicuous for their simplified representations of motifs, distortions of heightened expressiveness, and intensified colouring. Passionate pathos and unselfconscious spontaneity produced works that broke with the norms of a Pharisaic, self-satisfied bourgeois culture and also protested against the restrictive decorum of fashionable salon painting, official representative art and the Kitsch pseudo-realism of the day. Despite a similar starting point, the differences between "Brücke" and "Blue Rider" were clear-cut. Their reception was also very different, but it is hard to resist concluding that in Munich people were oriented to a much more international direction and aimed at a more rapid and more widely spread propagation of their aims. In this respect the love of Herwarth Walden for Marc and Kandinsky played a significant part. After he had founded the journal and publishing house called *Der Sturm* in Berlin in 1910, and added a gallery in 1912, Walden gave the Munich artists an important forum for spreading their ideas – one, moreover, which permitted them to establish contacts with the contemporary avant-garde in other countries. In addition, Marc and Kandinsky had a vision which, despite its ide-

which, despite its idealistic colouring, was aimed at revolutionary changes in society in which art was to show the way, indeed which it was to anticipate through its revolutionary forms of expression. The Brücke artists' scant verbal statements in favour of spiritual and aesthetic renewal are not readily discernible, nor do their works indicate anything of this synthesis of eschatalogical and utopian ideas. The fact that Kandinsky based his theory on quite obsolete traditions is a completely different matter. If it was Marc's intention to "create symbols of the times, which belong on the altars of a future spiritual religion and behind which their technical procreator disappears", statements of this kind emphasised the great distance between him and the Dresden artists. While people in Munich spoke of the spirit, the "Brücke" intended in the first instance to express what the artists felt, to depict "in an immediate and unadulterated" way what "drives the artist to create". The Dresden painters achieved an embodiment of free sensuality in a large number of paintings, something never attained by Marc or Kandinsky. This lay outside their world of ideas. Kirchner, Heckel and Schmidt-Rottluff never made the effort to transcend the horizon of direct experience. Sensuality and intellectualism, feeling and spirit, subjective sensation and objective striving – these are concepts highlighting the differences between "Brücke" and "Blue Rider". The contrast between the sensual-organic component of the Expressionists in Dresden, who as a true commune, developed a collective style for a time, and the endeavour of the more loosely connected Munich artists to make transcendent things visible in symbols through the metaphysical dematerialisation of reality – this antithesis was also manifest in the fact that Klee and Kandinsky, two ot the "Blue Rider" painters, obtained a constructive function in the State Bauhaus in Weimar and Dessau. Their theoretically founded art seemed to be teachable; the existential creativity of the "Brücke" was not.

EXPRESSIONIST GRAPHICS

HUBERTUS FRONING

THE beginnings of a radical change in art lay in rebellion and protest against conventional forces, long established mechanisms and conventional obligations which called new and assertive movements into being and brought them into conflict with society. The intensive, critical discussions about the problems and norms pertaining to that time set in train a search for new existential foundations whose genuineness and truth were manifest in an elemental, original desire for expression, a mirror of the unspoilt human being.

The artists of "Brücke" Expressionism, with their faith in the future, had intended to affect life and society through their art. The widespread impact they intended required special means of expression which had to be both aggressively insistent and formally constant. Printed graphics were not the only appropriate medium for realising these aims, but they were important from the artistic point of view for stimulating the creative powers of the artists.

From the beginning the artists favoured the woodcut, with its pronounced black-and-white contrasts, its sharp linear differentiation and its two-dimensional effect. It was a means of clarifying forms, since the resistance of the material forced them to conceive sparse shapes, as in no other medium. Heckel had always regarded printed graphics as a suitable medium for achieving a widespread impact – this is proven by the size of the editions of many of his woodcuts. Kirchner always did his printing himself in order to endow his works with an individual note. Schmidt-Rottluff, on the other hand, never recognised any prints he had not signed.

DR HUBERTUS FRONING
Chief Curator, Folkwang Museum, Essen

In their search for a new effect, determined by vivid qualities, the artists of the "Brücke" group found a formal precedent in the works of the Swiss artist Felix Valloton. They discerned a congenial attitude in his idiosyncratic style, which they adapted for their own woodcuts. Valloton derived his vocabulary from the multiplicity of styles of his time, placing pure white and pure black adjacent to each other for an intense effect.

When Emil Nolde became an active member in 1906, his artistic vitality was unmistakable. Kirchner acknowledged the stimulation: "His fantastic individuality gave the "Brücke" a new accent, he enriched our exhibitions with the interesting techniques of his etching and got to know those of our woodcuts". At first the broad, powerful etchings determined the structure of the pictures, but soon the artists were drawing directly onto the plate with a cold needle. Although it is in the nature of etching that the linear element predominates due to the scratching of the plate, the etchers organised the structure of their pictures by means of an arrangement of the surface in light-dark contrasts. Towards this effect, they incorporated the soft, muted tones of the partly etched plate. The positioning of the strokes, broadly laid out and concentrated into a unified dark surface, form lively areas of tension against the lightened tone of the plate. The single line, soft and swinging, mediates between the extremes of light and dark like a reconciling element. These artistic peculiarities gain even more atmospheric value in the early lithographs, which are freely painted onto the stone with a broad brush and tie the objects into a loose, spontaneously drawn structure.

Since the beginning of art, the representation of the nude has been a preferred theme, whether as studio exercise, as an autonomous work or as an integral feature of a landscape. The striving for immediacy and the demand for free naturalness instigated a completely new attitude to the model. For discipline, the artists drew from a live model, though not in the traditional way: the model had to change position every quarter of an hour. These so-called "quarter-hour nudes" were of great significance to their artistic development, since formal skills for the new art had first to be acquired. Studies from the model required a rapid grasp of a situation, demanding abbreviation and a particular certainty of feeling. The "quarter-hour nudes" are not only recorded in drawing, they also inspired the early graphics.

The artists displayed the same obsessive mania for work in this medium as they did in their drawing. There were occasions when, stimulated by the impressions of the day, they got up at night and reached for the wood block – sometimes it was the lid of a cigar-box – and carved out shapes with a gouge. Before day dawned, they had rolled the wood block, worked on the prints with a folding-tool and hung the prints on the wall. Alternatively, they would scratch their ideas for pictures into a zinc plate, which was cheaper than copper. Then again, they would run off a few prints from the lithographic stone so they could grind it down and draw on it again, with the result that sometimes the same flaw in the material appears in various works.

This manner of working led to a "hieroglyphic" shorthand marked by specific features of expression and a special kind of rhythm, particularly in the woodcuts: the surface of the wood block was torn open with a gouge in such a way that the splintered wood pieces, which had been deliberately retained, produced a splintery effect with a brittle, aggressive-looking structure.

The decision to depart from beautifully contoured lines, to dissolve form and make the marks suggestive caused an obvious discrepancy between this new art and the customary canon of beauty. Beauty or ugliness – and distortion is ugly in the traditional sense – were no longer significant criteria in the conception of this art. The new works possess their own aesthetic which cannot be measured by older criteria. The result was an increased tension between subjective attitudes and objective reality.

From 1909 onwards, a new boldness of outline can be observed in the treatment of form. The prints no longer followed the nervously fraying contours. The artists were now intent upon grasping the forms with few means and making bold use of empty spaces. They concentrated on the boldly placed line. With this approach, the influence of the Fauves, for example, Matisse, is evident.

One virtuoso example of this broadly outlined treatment is Schmidt-Rottluff's woodcut *Villa with Tower* (1911). By way of the destruction of form in the two previous versions of this theme, the third one, contains a clarification. The tower in the background is cut like an arrow pointing upwards. The straight-line contours and gentle bow shapes give the print a restrained tension. The calculated, emphatically formalised structure dominates a visionary apparition. A great desire for order characterises each individual picture.

The rejection of detailed, differentiated small pieces and the bold use of empty spaces can also be demonstrated in Heckel's woodcut *Woman reclining* (1909). The picture gains life from the strong colour contrast of black, red and blue, and the effect of flat forms. The irregular white lines dividing the colours are technically determined by the printing process. Heckel did not print from several blocks but sawed the prepared uncut wood, applied colour to the individual parts and put them together again for the printing. The result is not accidental, but deliberately intended by the artist. The singularity of this technique, which renewed the woodcut tradition, was already practised by Edvard Munch.

The new printing process accommodating these artistic intentions, emphasises the two dimensionality and extremely strong intensity of the colour and it emphasises the contrast between the figure and the abstract background. As a result of the stress on the surface, the empirical time-space relationships remain indeterminate, the concrete is transformed from particularity into generalisation. Colour does not serve the material definition of certain objects nor describe their substance, but maintains its own sensuous quality and is oriented towards the total effect. In its emblematic effect it also emphasises the distortion of the figure.

The recourse to flatness in the woodcut, which

became a conventional feature of art from 1909 onwards, also introduced the so-called "hard" style, which was stimulated by, among other things, carvings from the Palau Islands east of the Philippines. The "Brücke" artists had seen carvings in the Dresden Museum of Ethnography – numerous, mostly mythological figures carved on roofing timber cross beams – and had been struck by their power of expression and vivacity; the hard nature of the material is such that round or cursive forms are pre-empted.

The Expressionists' orientation to so-called primitive art was not merely a matter of style: it also meant an escape from the social reality of the "established forces" and was a protest against the false belief in progress of a dehumanized industrial society. Their declaration in favour of primitivism was intended to uncover again the buried natural powers of human potential.

The artists aspired to the primitive creative energy they saw reflected in African and South Sea Island art, searching for it in the solitude of nature – which meant, for them, an escape from society. They discovered picturesque places a long way from the large cities on the coasts of the Baltic and the North Sea. Apart from the coastal towns Dangast, Nidden, Prerow and the island of Fehmarn, they loved the Moritzburg Lakes near Dresden. Among their favourite themes were the nude in nature, bathers on the beach and nudes among the dunes. The nude in a natural environment was considered to express the liberation of the physical life from the narrow moral ideas of the time, a rejection of out-dated values. In this endeavour,

KARL SCHMIDT-ROTTLUFF
Villa with tower – 1911
Woodcut Cat. 94
Museum Folkwang, Essen

the natural poses of the models accorded with the spontaneity of artistic creation.

Between 1908 and 1911, all the artists had moved to Berlin. The reason for moving to the metropolis was that conservative Dresden, where they had lived until then, was probably unable to provide them with a livelihood on account of lack of interest. The population of Berlin, on the other hand, was much less prejudiced and more open-minded. The city offered the opportunity to make contacts, for it attracted many artists who were struggling for a new feeling for life. This is how Feininger came into the "Brücke" circle in 1912, through his friendship with Schmidt-Rottluff and Heckel. Feininger's *Tor (The Gate)* dates from that year; it was the expression of an inner emotion, changing the external world into a subjective experience. Even the heavens were included in the crystalline structure of the background. The resemblance to Cubism was still quite close, and the adaptation of this style resulted in much more unified compositions in the later woodcuts, which began with the assumption that the wooden surface was two dimensional. Fields torn up, forms splintered, blocks colliding and layered energetically, full of explosive forces – all these subordinate themselves to a strict desire for form. In the metropolis, the "Brücke" artists also turned to other themes. Their attitudes were far removed from bourgeois life, and they adopted an outsider's position in this sense as well. Questions of content increasingly preoccupied them; a sign of their critical approach to the problems of their time.

Dance, variety theatre, cocottes and the circus were metaphors for life in the metropolis which fascinated the Expressionist artists. Even a conservative thinker like Oswald Spengler was unable to resist the magic of the metropolis: "Anyone who has ever come under the spell of the whole sinful beauty of this last miracle of history will never free himself from it."

Kirchner's street paintings mirrored the experience of the metropolis in an exemplary way: the cocottes symbolised the decadence and vulnerability of urban life. In the woodcut, the artist used sharp, narrow wedges, broken contours and great contrasts of brightness. The intensification of the emotions to a state of excitement is achieved by hatching, which opens up the black and white forms and produces a flickering and vibrating appearance appropriate to the theme.

In one lithograph, Kirchner depicted the *Cake Walk*, an American Negro dance which rapidly entered the repertoire of the variety theatre. The synchronized postures of the dancers created the impression of regulated movement, despite the verve of the drawing. The marionette-like, angular, rhythmic dance led to a precarious construction stabilized by bold colours. Nolde, on the other hand, in his *Candle Dancers* stressed the ecstatic, abandoned, intoxicated aspects of the dance through the acute slant of the figures, which almost had them tipping out of the frame. Nolde spoke of a primaeval life of nature that he wished to depict. What the artists invoked as the immediacy of artistic creation, as the free feeling of life, as naturalness, appears in the guise of the ecstatic dance, which was seen as more than an aesthetic sequence of movements. It was a life liberated from all intellectual fetters, universally comprehensible and immediate, because it represented the possibility of spontaneous expression,

In the meantime, the collective style had outlived itself. The individual peculiarities of each of the artists re-emerged during World War I, for what occupied the foreground was no longer the liberation of creative forces but a suffering and driven humanity, and occasionally also its salvation. In this period, it was the black and white starkness of the woodcut, which rejects all superfluity and all attempts to please, that many artists saw as a token of some kind of faith urging them to convey a message. Their own loss of identity also required expression, as in Kirchner's illustrations to Chamisso's story *Peter Schlemihl* (the story of a man who sells his shadow to the Devil – translator's note), which Gustav Schiefler, that great connoisseur of the Expressionists, called the "life story of a man suffering from persecution mania,... of a man who, as the result of some event suddenly becomes aware of his infinite smallness".

There were special numbers of the journal *Die Aktion (Action)* from 1916 to 1918 which were related to the War: *Peace on Earth, Christmas 1917* and *Golgotha*. Schmidt-Rottluff produced a series of representations of Christ in 1918 which features this theme most emphatically. All the motifs have been reduced to brief, hieroglyphic notations, mostly defined by angular lines. The main figures have been foregrounded as large silhouettes.

Beckmann dramatised the Fall as a hard, disillusioned image of horror. He deploys close-ups and distortion to express overwhelming tensions.

For Rohlfs, a comparable theme, *The Expulsion from Paradise* is an image of being abandoned to die. The cowering human couple becomes an expression of spiritual despair resulting from an act they have committed. In the picture *The Captive*, also by Rohlfs, anxiety, despair and hopelessness are condensed in a human face which is a mirror of the tragic manifestation of man, an expression of the depths of his being. Against the background of the War, other themes also gain explosive force. None could be better suited to call back a mankind thought lost, to exhort it to reflect upon itself, to turn around, than the *Prodigal Son*. The patriarchal father bends lovingly over the wretched figure of the son to hear his confession and to take the outcast back into the family. The Christian message here contains the seeds of salvation.

Heckel's was the only work that the War did not radically change in the range of subjects. As a first-aid orderly he had direct experience of the suffering of the soldiers, but his art showed few of these horrors. Evidently it was not in Heckel's nature to become a socially critical artist. Schiefler reports that he was more dedicated to relieving the terrible hours of the wounded, the convalescent and dying. From 1914, he sought to bring the psychological tensions of the early period into a balanced, orderly synthesis. The bold outline, stressing the strength of the picture, replaced the formerly splintered surface and frayed contours. Such is the case in *Crouching woman* (1914), and it attains a dignified, mature expression in *Man's Head* (1919). Here Heckel consolidates the strictly controlled flow of the lines, which stands in a curious relationship of tension to the large, bold surfaces. The intellectual discipline of the artist holds together the polarities of surface and structural line, as though their unity were self-evident.

Not all the artists who worked in the post-war period affected the same reconciliation in the language of form and in their subject-matter. The War drove Grosz to an unlimited scorn for humanity, and he stylised his work with harshness, brutality, an outspokenness that hurt. For him, art became a safety valve for inner tensions, and exposed and unmasked dreams and lusts. In bewildering variety, he hurled the spectacular wealth of his experiences onto the rectangle of the picture, sketchily, without any organisation of depth. The figures were drawn in simple outline: they have lost their balance and fallen into relationships by association. The hardness, even ruthlessness of the lithographic lines reflected a world in ruins. The grim sarcasm of Dix was no different. In *Sketch*, a print of evocative power, Dix used the engraving needle like a scalpel. Influenced by Dada, the figure became a mechanical prop, obedient to stimuli and orders like a puppet.

The prints of the twenties were connected to current events. Although they retained points of contact with the declaredly expressive and emotive art of the previous era, they also anticipated the development of future graphics, whose forms were determined solely by a spirit of opposition.

CATALOGUE

MAX BECKMANN
Frauenbad – 1919 *(Women's Bath)*
Oil on canvas
97.5 x 66 cm
Staatliche Museen Preussischer Kulturbesitz, Nationalgalerie, Berlin
Cat. 1

MAX BECKMANN
Duchessa di Malvedi – 1926 *(Duchess of Malvedi)*
Oil on canvas
66.5 x 27 cm
Bayerische Staatsgemäldesammlungen, Munich – Staatsgalerie
moderner Kunst
Cat. 2

MAX BECKMANN
Neapel, Vesuv – 1926 (Naples, Mt Vesuvius)
Oil on canvas
85.5 x 24.4 cm
Bayerische Staatsgemäldesammlungen, Munich – Staatsgalerie
moderner Kunst
Cat. 3

MAX BECKMANN
Sinnende Frau am Meer – 1936/37 *(Pensive woman by the sea)*
Oil on canvas
65.5 x 110.5 cm
Kunsthalle, Bremen
Cat. 4

OTTO DIX
Der Traum – 1914 *(The Dream)*
Oil on canvas
65 x 57.5 cm
Museum Folkwang, Essen
Cat. 5

OTTO DIX
Arbeiterjunge – 1920 *(Young worker)*
Oil on panel
86 x 40.8 cm
Galerie der Stadt Stuttgart
Cat. 6

LYONEL FEININGER
Am Quai – 1912 (*At the quay*)
Oil on canvas
40.5 x 48 cm
Sprengel Museum Hannover
Cat. 7

LYONEL FEININGER
Leuchtbarke 1 – c1913 (Lighthouse I)
Oil on canvas
105 x 91 cm
Museum Folkwang, Essen
Cat. 8

LYONEL FEININGER
Kirche im Niedergrundstedt – 1919 *(Church of Niedergrundstedt)*
Oil on canvas
101 x 125 cm
Staatliche Museen Preussischer Kulterbesitz, Nationalgalerie, Berlin
Cat. 9

LYONEL FEININGER
Der Rote Turm von Halle – 1930 *(The Red Tower of Halle)*
Oil on canvas
101 x 81 cm
Städtisches Museum, Mulheim
Cat. 10

ERICH HECKEL
Die Elbe bei Dresden – 1905 *(The Elbe near Dresden)*
Oil on canvas
51 x 70 cm
Museum Folkwang, Essen
Cat. 11

ERICH HECKEL
Häuser bei Rom – 1909 (Houses in Rome)
Oil on canvas
69 x 74 cm
Private collection, Federal Republic of Germany
Cat. 12

ERICH HECKEL
Landschaft auf Alsen – 1913 *(Landscape of Alsen)*
Oil on canvas
83.5 x 91 cm
Museum Folkwang, Essen
Cat. 13

ERICH HECKEL
Aus einem Irrenhaus – 1914 *(In a lunatic asylum)*
Oil on canvas
70.5 x 80.5 cm
Städtisches Museum Gelsenkirchen, Gelsenkirchen-Buer
Cat. 14

ALEXEJ VON JAWLENSKY
Bretonisches Mädchen – 1910 *(Breton girl)*
Oil on cardboard
64 x 46 cm
Leopold-Hoesch-Museum der Stadt, Duren
Cat. 15

ALEXEJ VON JAWLENSKY
Stilleben mit Früchten – c1910 *(Still life with fruit)*
Oil on canvas
48 x 67.7 cm
Städtische Galerie im Lenbachhaus, Munich
Cat. 16

ALEXEJ VON JAWLENSKY
Hügel – 1912 *(Hill)*
Oil on cardboard
53.5 x 64 cm
Museum Am Ostwall, Dortmund
Cat 17.

ALEXEJ VON JAWLENSKY
Spanierin mit Spitzenschal – 1913 (*Spanish woman*
with lace mantilla)
Oil on paperboard
68 x 47.7 cm
Private collection, Federal Republic of Germany
Cat. 18

WASSILY KANDINSKY
Studie zu Komposition VII – 1913 (*Study for Composition VII*)
Oil on canvas
78 x 99.5 cm
Städtische Galerie im Lenbachhaus, Munich
Cat. 19

WASSILY KANDINSKY
Unbenannte Improvisation IV – 1914
(Untitled Improvisation IV)
Oil on canvas
124.5 x 73.5 cm
Städtische Galerie im Lenbachhaus, Munich
Cat. 20

ERNST LUDWIG KIRCHNER
Ins Meer Schreitende – 1912 *(Striding into the sea)*
Oil on canvas
146 x 200 cm
Staatsgalerie Stuttgart
Cat. 21

ERNST LUDWIG KIRCHNER
Bootshafen auf Fehmarn – 1913 *(Boat Harbour, Fehmarn)*
Oil on canvas
65.5 x 96.7 cm
Kunsthalle, Bremen
Cat. 22

ERNST LUDWIG KIRCHNER
Drei Badende – 1913 *(Three bathers)*
Oil on canvas
197.5 x 147.5 cm
Art Gallery of New South Wales, Sydney First Foundation purchase 1984
Cat. 23

ERNST LUDWIG KIRCHNER
Frauen beim Tee: die Kranke – 1914 (Women at tea:
The sick woman)
Oil on canvas
100.5 x 76 cm
Bayerische Staatsgemäldesammlungen, Munich – Staatsgalerie
moderner Kunst
Cat. 24

ERNST LUDWIG KIRCHNER
Leipziger Strasse – 1914 *(Leipzig Street)*
Oil on canvas
71.2 x 87 cm
Museum Folkwang, Essen
Cat. 25

OSKAR KOKOSCHKA
Die Verkündigung – 1911 *(The Annunciation)*
Oil on canvas
83 x 122.5 cm
Museum Am Ostwall, Dortmund
Cat. 26

OSKAR KOKOSCHKA
Venezianische Szene – 1912 *(Venetian scene)*
Oil on canvas
60 x 76 cm
Kunstmuseum Düsseldorf
Cat. 27

AUGUST MACKE
Gemüsefelder – 1911 *(Vegetable fields)*
Oil on canvas
47.5 x 64 cm
Städtisches Kunstmuseum Bonn
Cat. 28

AUGUST MACKE
Die Frau des Künstlers – 1912 (*The artist's wife*)
Oil on canvas
105 x 81 cm
Staatliche Museen Preussischer Kulturbesitz, Nationalgalerie, Berlin
Cat. 29

AUGUST MACKE
Mädchen am Springbrunnen – 1913 *(Girls at the fountain)*
Oil on canvas
142 x 73.5 cm
Westfälisches Landesmuseum für Kunst und Kultergeschichte, Munster
Cat. 30

FRANZ MARC
Kleine Blaue Pferde – 1911 *(The small Blue Horses)*
Oil on canvas
61.5 x 101 cm
Staatsgalerie Stuttgart
Cat. 31

OTTO MUELLER
Zwei sitzende Akte – (Two seated nudes)
Oil on canvas
84 x 100.5 cm
Westfälisches Landesmuseum für Kunst und Kulturgeschichte, Munster
Cat. 32

OTTO MUELLER
Badende im Schilfgraben – 1914 *(Bathers in the rushes)*
Oil on canvas
92 x 79 cm
Staatliche Museen Preussischer Kulturbesitz, Nationalgalerie, Berlin
Cat. 33

OTTO MUELLER
Maschka mit Maske – 1919/21 *(Maschka with mask)*
Distemper on hessian
95.8 x 67.5 cm
Museum Folkwang, Essen
Cat 34.

GABRIELE MÜNTER
*Murnau vom Griesbräufenster aus – 1908 (Murnau trom the Griesbräu
window)*
Oil on canvas
32.5 x 40.8 cm
Städtische Galerie im Lenbachhaus, Munich
Cat. 35

GABRIELE MÜNTER
Stilleben mit Sessel – 1909 *(Still life with chair)*
Oil on canvas
72.5 x 49 cm
Städtische Galerie im Lenbachhaus, Munich
Cat. 36

EMIL NOLDE
Frau in Blumengarten – 1907 (*Woman in flower garden*)
Oil on canvas
63 x 78.5 cm
Karl Ernst Osthaus Museum, Hagen
Cat. 37

EMIL NOLDE
Im Cafe – 1911 *(In the cafe)*
Oil on canvas
73 x 89 cm
Museum Folkwang, Essen
Cat. 38

EMIL NOLDE
Freies Meer – 1918 *(Open sea)*
Oil on canvas
86.4 x 100 cm
Museum Folkwang, Essen
Cat. 39

EMIL NOLDE
Puppen und Papagai – c1919 *(Dolls and parrot)*
Oil on canvas
46.5 x 59.5 cm
Bayerische Staatsgemäldesammlungen, Munich – Staatsgalerie
moderner Kunst
Cat. 40

MAX PECHSTEIN
Flusslandschaft – c1907 *(River landscape)*
Oil on canvas
53 x 68 cm
Museum Folkwang, Essen
Cat. 41

MAX PECHSTEIN
Rotes Mädchen am Tisch – 1910 *(Red girl at the table)*
Oil on canvas
75 x 75.5 cm
Museum Folkwang, Essen
Cat. 42

81

MAX PECHSTEIN
Am Strand von Nidden – 1911 *(On the beach of Nidden)*
Oil on canvas
50 x 65 cm
Staatliche Museen Preussischer Kulturbesitz, Nationalgalerie, Berlin
Cat. 43

CHRISTIAN ROHLFS
St Patroklos in Soest – c1906
Oil on canvas
115 x 75 cm
Museum Folkwang, Essen
Cat. 44

CHRISTIAN ROHLFS
Tanz um den Sonnenball – 1914 *(Dance around the fireball)*
Tempera on canvas
100 x 125 cm
Städtische Kunsthalle, Recklinghausen
Cat. 45

CHRISTIAN ROHLFS
Akrobaten – c1916 *(Acrobats)*
Oil on canvas
110 x 75.5 cm
Museum Folkwang, Essen
Cat. 46

KARL SCHMIDT-ROTTLUFF
Dorfecke – 1910 *(Village corner)*
Oil on canvas
87 x 95 cm
Brücke-Museum, Berlin. Donated by Karl and Emy Schmidt-Rottluff-Stiftung
Cat. 47

KARL SCHMIDT-ROTTLUFF
Fischerkahne auf dem Haff – 1913 *(Fishing boats on the lagoon)*
Oil on canvas
88 x 101 cm
Museum Folkwang, Essen
Cat.48

KARL SCHMIDT-ROTTLUFF
Frau und Mädchen – c1920 *(Woman and girl)*
Oil on canvas
101 x 87.5 cm
Bayerische Staatsgemäldesammlungen, Munich – Staatsgalerie moderner Kunst
Cat. 49

MAX BECKMANN
Adam und Eva – 1917
(Adam and Eve)
Drypoint
23.1 x 17.1 cm
Museum Folkwang, Essen
Cat. 50

MAX BECKMANN
Selbstbildnis mit Zigarette – 1919
(Self-portrait with cigarette)
Drypoint
23.5 x 19.7 cm
Museum Folkwang, Essen
Cat. 51

MAX BECKMANN
Grosse Brücke – 1922
(Large bridge)
Drypoint
42.5 x 25.7 cm
Museum Folkwang, Essen
Cat. 52

MAX BECKMANN
Tamerlan – 1923
Drypoint
39.6 x 20 cm
Museum Folkwang, Essen
Cat. 53

OTTO DIX
Sketch – 1922
Etching
39.5 x 29.6 cm
Museum Folkwang, Essen
Cat. 54

OTTO DIX
Verächter des Todes – 1922
(Dare devils)
Drypoint
34.5 x 27.5 cm
Museum Folkwang, Essen
Cat. 55

OTTO DIX
Manitschka – 1923
Lithograph
35.2 x 29 cm
Museum Folkwang, Essen
Cat. 56

OTTO DIX
Bildnis Frau Otto Mueller – 1923
(Portrait of Mrs Otto Mueller)
Lithograph
49 x 38.5 cm
Museum Folkwang, Essen
Cat. 57

LYONEL FEININGER
The Gate – 1912
Etching
27 x 20 cm
Museum Folkwang, Essen
Cat. 58

LYONEL FEININGER
Gelmeroda II – 1918
Woodcut
28.5 x 23.2 cm
Museum Folkwang, Essen
Cat. 59

LYONEL FEININGER
Daasdorf – 1918
Woodcut
33 x 45 cm
Museum Folkwang, Essen
Cat. 60

LYONEL FEININGER
Benz – 1919
Woodcut
21.3 x 29.1 cm
Museum Folkwang, Essen
Cat. 61

GEORG GROSZ
Eva – 1918
(Eve)
Lithograph
30 x 21.5 cm
Museum Folkwang, Essen
Cat. 62

GEORG GROSZ
Emigrantencafe Wolga-Wolga
(Emigrant cafe, Wolga-Wolga)
Lithograph
49 x 34.7 cm
Museum Folkwang, Essen
Cat. 63

GEORG GROSZ
Strassenszene
(Street scene)
Lithograph
52.6 x 38.3 cm
Museum Folkwang, Essen
Cat. 64

GEORG GROSZ
Verzweiflung
(Despair)
Lithograph
70.5 x 53.7 cm
Museum Folkwang, Essen
Cat. 65

ERICH HECKEL
Liegende – 1909
(Woman reclining)
Woodcut
40 x 29.9 cm
Museum Folkwang, Essen
Cat. 66

ERICH HECKEL
Weisse Pferde – 1912
(White horses)
Colour woodcut
31 x 31.2 cm
Museum Folkwang, Essen
Cat. 67

ERICH HECKEL
Hockende – 1914
(Crouching woman)
Woodcut
41.4 x 30.7 cm
Museum Folkwang, Essen
Cat. 68

ERICH HECKEL
Männerkopf – 1919
(Man's head)
Colour woodcut
46.1 x 32.7 cm
Museum Folkwang, Essen
Cat. 69

ERNST LUDWIG KIRCHNER
Artistenkind – 1907
(Artist's child)
Lithograph
38.3 x 32.9 cm
Museum Folkwang, Essen
Cat. 70

ERNST LUDWIG KIRCHNER
Rappenhengst, Reiterin und Clown – 1907
(Black stallion, rider and clown)
Colour lithograph
59 x 51 cm
Museum Folkwang, Essen
Cat. 71

ERNST LUDWIG KIRCHNER
Cake-Walk – 1911
Colour lithograph
34 x 39 cm
Museum Folkwang, Essen
Cat. 72

ERNST LUDWIG KIRCHNER
Schlemihls Begegnung mit dem Schatten
(Schlemihl's encounter with the shadow)
Colour woodcut
30.5 x 29.8 cm
Museum Folkwang, Essen
Cat. 73

OSKAR KOKOSCHKA
Sitzendes Mädchen
(Seated girl)
Lithograph
40.5 x 55.5 cm
Museum Folkwang, Essen
Cat. 74

OSKAR KOKOSCHKA
Frauenbildnis – c1924
(Portrait of a woman)
Lithograph
51 x 38.4 cm
Museum Folkwang, Essen
Cat. 75

OSKAR KOKOSCHKA
Frauenbildnis – c1924
(Portrait of a woman)
Lithograph
69.3 x 43.4 cm
Museum Folkwang, Essen
Cat. 76

OTTO MUELLER
Fünf Akte
(Five nudes)
Colour lithograph
33.5 x 43.5 cm
Museum Folkwang, Essen
Cat. 77

OTTO MUELLER
Selbstbildnis
(Self-portrait)
Lithograph
40.2 x 28.5 cm
Museum Folkwang, Essen
Cat. 78

OTTO MUELLER
Hockende Akte
(Crouching nudes)
Lithograph
28.7 x 38.6 cm
Museum Folkwang, Essen
Cat. 79

OTTO MUELLER
Zigeunerfamilie
(Gypsy family)
Lithograph
25.9 x 18.8 cm
Museum Folkwang, Essen
Cat. 80

EMIL NOLDE
Tingel-Tangel II – 1907
(Honky Tonk II)
Colour lithograph
43 x 61 cm
Museum Folkwang, Essen
Cat. 81

EMIL NOLDE
Hamburger Schiff im Dock – 1910
(Hamburg ship at dock)
Etching
31 x 41 cm
Museum Folkwang, Essen
Cat. 82

EMIL NOLDE
Die Hlg. drei Könige – 1913
(The three Magi)
Colour lithograph
75 x 64 cm
Museum Folkwang, Essen
Cat. 83

EMIL NOLDE
Kerzentänzerin – 1917
(Candle dancers)
Woodcut
30 x 23.5 cm
Museum Folkwang, Essen
Cat. 84

MAX PECHSTEIN
Variete – 1909
(Vaudeville)
Colour lithograph
28 x 37.7 cm
Museum Folkwang, Essen
Cat. 85

MAX PECHSTEIN
Weiblicher Kopf II – 1909
(Female head II)
Lithograph
43 x 32 cm
Museum Folkwang, Essen
Cat. 86

MAX PECHSTEIN
Landschaft mit Kühen – 1919
(Landscape with cows)
Woodcut
31.8 x 39.9 cm
Museum Folkwang, Essen
Cat. 87

MAX PECHSTEIN
Zwiesprache – 1920
(Dialogue)
Colour woodcut
40 x 31.9 cm
Museum Folkwang, Essen
Cat. 88

CHRISTIAN ROHLFS
Geist Gottes uber den Wassern – 1915
(The Spirit of God over the waters)
Woodcut
55.4 x 46.3 cm
Museum Folkwang, Essen
Cat. 89

CHRISTIAN ROHLFS
Der verlorene Sohn – 1916
(The Prodigal son)
Woodcut
49.3 x 35.6 cm
Museum Folkwang, Essen
Cat. 90

CHRISTIAN ROHLFS
Austreibung aus dem Paradies – 1917
(Expulsion from Paradise)
Woodcut
53.4 x 68.8 cm
Museum Folkwang, Essen
Cat. 91

CHRISTIAN ROHLFS
Der Gefangene – 1918
(The captive)
Woodcut
64.6 x 51.4 cm
Museum Folkwang, Essen
Cat. 92

KARL SCHMIDT-ROTTLUFF
Akt – 1909
(Nude)
Woodcut
39.8 x 24.9 cm
Museum Folkwang, Essen
Cat. 93

KARL SCHMIDT-ROTTLUFF
Villa mit Turm – 1911
(Villa with tower)
Woodcut
50 x 39.4 cm
Museum Folkwang, Essen
Cat. 94

KARL SCHMIDT-ROTTLUFF
Russischer Wald – 1918
(Russian forest)
Woodcut
19.7 x 25.9 cm
Museum Folkwang, Essen
Cat. 95

KARL SCHMIDT-ROTTLUFF
Gang nach Emmaus – 1918
(The road to Emmaus)
Woodcut
30 x 39.8 cm
Museum Folkwang, Essen
Cat. 96

BIOGRAPHIES

MAX BECKMANN

Born 12.2.1884 in Leipzig, died 27.12.1950 in New York. 1899-1903 at the Art School in Weimar. 1903-04 stay in Paris. 1906 exhibition in the Berlin Secession, of which he was a member from 1908-11. Medical orderly in Belgium and Holland. 1915-33 resident in Frankfurt, where he conducted the painting classes at the Art School. 1933 removed from office by the National Socialists, moved to Berlin. 1937, emigrated to Amsterdam. 1937-38 resident in Paris, 1938-47 in Amsterdam again. 1947, emigrated to the USA. From 1949 teaching activity in the Brooklyn Museum in New York. 1950, received the Carnegie Prize and the prize of the Biennale in Venice.

OTTO DIX

Born 2.12.1891 in Untermhaus (Thuringia), died 25.7.1969 in Singen. 1905-1910 apprenticeship as an interior decorator. Subsequently, studied at the College of Arts and Crafts in Dresden and at the Art Academy under Richard Müller. Military service from 1914-18. Continued his studies in Dresden from 1919- 21. 1919 co-founder of the "Group 19". 1922-25, studied at the Düsseldorf Academy and free-lance artist. Joined the group "Young Rhineland". to which Max Ernst also belonged. 1925-27 in Berlin. 1927 appointment to the Dresden Academy. Removed from office by the National Socialists. 1935 moved to Hemmenhofen on Lake Constance. 1945, military service again, 1946-47 French prisoner of war. 1950 teaching post at the Düsseldorf Academy. 1959 awarded the Order of the FRG.

LYONEL FEININGER

Born 17.7.1871 in New York, died 13.1.1956 also in New York. 1887 moved to Germany. 1888 studied at the School of Arts and Crafts in Hamburg. 1889-92 studied at the Berlin Academy. 1892-93 at the Atelier Colarossi in Paris. 1894-1906 worked as a caricaturist for German and American magazines. Turned to painting in 1905. 1906 with Colarossi in Paris again. 1908 returned to Berlin. 1911 travelled to Paris, interested in Cubism. 1913 took part in the "Blue Rider" exhibition in Berlin. 1917 exhibition in the Gallery of "Der Sturm" brought him a breakthrough as a painter. 1919-1933 taught in the Bauhaus in Weimar and Dessau. 1924 co-founder of the group "The Blue Four". Denounced by the National Socialists as "degenerate". 1936 emigrated to the USA. Teaching appointments at Mills College in California and the Black Mountain College in North Carolina.

GEORG GROSZ

Born 26.7.1893 in Berlin, died there on 6.7.1959. 1909 studied at the Dresden Academy, continuing 1916 in Berlin under Emil Orlik. Brief military service. 1918, co-founder of the Berlin Dada movement. 1919 co-editor of several political-satirical journals, e.g. "Die Pleite" (Gone Broke) and "Der blutige Ernst" (Bloody Ernest). 1920 participation in the "International Dada Fair" in Berlin. Between 1922 and 1928 trips to Russia, France and Switzerland. 1925, occasionally joined the "New Sobriety". 1932 Guest Teacher at the Art Students League of New York. 1933 moved to the USA. 1941-42 teaching post at Columbia University. Returned to Berlin in 1959, the year of his death.

ERICH HECKEL

Born 21.7.1883 in Döbeln, Saxony, died 27.1.1970 in Hemmenhofen (on Lake Constance). 1904, studied architecture at the Technical University, Dresden. 1905 Co-founder of the Artists' Group "Die Brücke", whose business manager and secretary he was. 1907-08 at Dangast on the North Sea with Schmidt-Rottluff. 1909 journey to Italy, with Kirchner at the Moritzburg Lakes near Dresden. 1911 with Jawlensky at Prerow on the Baltic. Moved to Berlin, joined the Berlin Secession. 1912 met Macke and Feininger, participated in the "Sonderbund"-exhibition in Cologne. 1913 one-man exhibitions in Berlin. 1915-18 medical orderly in Flanders, where he met Beckmann and Ensor. 1918, returned to Berlin. Various trips around Europe between 1921 to 1945. Defamed by the Nazis as "degenerate". 1944, moved to Hemmenhofen. 1949 teaching position at the College of Fine Arts, Karlsruhe.

ALEXEI JAWLENSKY

Born 13.3.1864 in Kuslowo (Russia), died 15.3.1941 in Wiesbaden. Military training in Moscow from 1877. Studied at the St. Petersburg Academy 1879. 1896 moved to Munich, joined Anton Azbè's school of painting, meeting with Kandinsky. 1903-05 travelled in Brittany and Provence. Took part in the exhibitions of the Secessions in Munich and Berlin. 1906 exhibition in the Salon d'Automne. 1907 in Matisse's atelier. 1909 member of the "New Artists' Association of Munich". 1914 moved to Switzerland, from 1921 resident in Wiesbaden. 1924 co-founder of the group "The Blue Four". 1929 contracted arthritis deformans, and partially paralysed. Denounced by the National Socialists as "degenerate". Prohibited from exhibiting from 1933, his works confiscated in 1937. 1938 his illness forced him to stop painting.

WASSILY KANDINSKY

Born 4.12.1866 in Moscow, died 13,12.1944 in Neuilly-sur-Seine near Paris. 1886-92 studied law and economics in Moscow. 1896 moved to Munich. 1897 joined the painting school of Anton Azbè. 1900 changed to the Academy, student of Franz von Stuck. Until 1903 a teacher in the private art school of the artists association "Phalanx", its president until 1904. Until 1908, numerous journeys in Europe and North Africa, at the same time, took part in exhibitions, e.g. the Berlin Secession 1902, the Salon d'Automne 1904, the "Brücke" 1906. From 1908 lived alternately in Murnau and Munich. 1909 co-founder of the "New Artists' Association of Munich" and its president. 1911 co-founder of the group "The Blue Rider". 1914, returned to Moscow. 1918 appointment to the Moscow Academy. 1920 Chair at the University of Moscow. 1922-33 teaching appointment at the Bauhaus in Weimar and Dresden. 1933 moved to Neuilly-sur-Seine, French citizen from 1939.

ERNST LUDWIG KIRCHNER

Born 6.5.1880 in Aschaffenburg, suicided 15.6.1938 in Frauenkirch near Davos, Switzerland. Began an architecture course at the Technical University, Dresden in 1901. 1903 spent two semesters at the "Ateliers for Teaching and Research" for applied and fine arts in Munich. 1905 completed his architecture course in Dresden. Co-founder of the Artists' Group "Die Brücke". 1910 member of the "New Secession" in Berlin. 1911 moved to Berlin, took up contact with the journal *Der Sturm*. 1912 took part in the Sonderbund exhibition in Cologne. 1914 military service. After a complete collapse, long stay in a sanatorium in the Taunus Mountains. 1917 moved to Davos, resident in Frauenkirch from 1923. Worked with the weaver Lisa Gujer. 1931 member of the Prussian Academy of the Graphic Arts. 1933 Kirchner retrospective in Berne, while at the same time his works were regarded as "degenerate" in Germany.

OSKAR KOKOSCHKA

Born 1.3.1886 in Pöchlarn, near Vienna, died 22.2.1980 in Montreux. 1905-09 at the School of Arts and Crafts in Vienna. 1907 worked with the "Wiener Werkstätte" (Vienna Workshops producing very modern items for every day use). 1910 contributor to the journal *Der Sturm*. 1911, returned to Vienna. His main activities in Germany until 1913, included exhibition in the Berlin Secession, the Sonderbund in Cologne, the New Secession in Munich and one-man show in Berlin. 1913, Italian journey. 1914 military service in the War, 1916 wounded at the Russian front. 1918 moved to Dresden, where he taught at the Academy from 1919-24. 1924, gave up his position and travelled through the Mediterranean countries. 1931 moved to Vienna, 1934 emigrated to Prague. 1938 escaped to London. 1948-49 stayed in Italy. Until 1954 in London again, then moved to Switzerland. In the meantime, he also lived in Salzburg, where he taught from 1953 to 1963 at the "School of Seeing" which he co-founded at the International Summer Academy for the Graphic Arts.

AUGUST MACKE

Born 3.1.1887 in Meschede on the Ruhr, killed in action 26.9.1914 in Champagne. 1904-06 studied at the Düsseldorf Academy. Position as stage designer. 1905 journey to Italy, 1906 to Holland, Belgium and London, 1907 to Paris. 1909-10 sojourn at Lake Tegern, Bavaria, meeting with Marc. Contacts with the "New Artists' Association of Munich". 1911 sojourned with Moilliet in Thun (Switzerland) and with Marc in Sindelsdorf. Member of the "Blue Rider" Group. 1912 moved to Bonn, participated in the Sonderbund exhibition in Cologne. In autumn 1912 in Paris with Marc. Organized the 1913 special exhibition of Rhineland Expressionists and avant-garde artists in Cologne. Winter 1913/14 meeting with Delaunay near Lake Thun. Moved to Switzerland. 1914 journeyed with Moilliet and Klee to Tunis. Began military service in August.

FRANZ MARC

Born 8.2.1880 in Munich, killed in action 4.3.1916 near Verdun. After breaking off his studies in philosophy and theology, at the Munich Art Academy, travelled to Italy in 1902. 1903 trip to Paris and Brittany. From 1904, free-lance artist in Upper Bavaria. 1907, second stay in Paris. 1909, member of the "New Artists' Association". 1911 foundation member of the group "The Blue Rider". 1912 publications in the journal of this name. Trip with Macke to

Paris, meeting with Delaunay. Took part in the organization of the first German Autumn Salon in Berlin. 1914 moved to Ried near Benediktbeuren and began military service.

OTTO MUELLER

Born 16.10.1874 in Liebau (Silesia), died 24.9.1930 in Breslau. 1890-94 apprentice lithographer in Görlitz. 1894-96 studied at the Academy in Dresden. 1896-97 travelled with his cousin Gerhart Hauptmann (the famous writer) to Italy and Switzerland. In 1898-99 continued his studies at the Munich Academy. Worked as a free-lance artist in Dresden. Spent time in the Riesengebirge (mountains), in Bohemia and the environs of Dresden. 1908, moved to Berlin. 1910-13 member of the artists group "Die Brücke". 1911 exhibition of the New Secession. 1911-12 summer trips to Bohemia with Kirchner. 1915-18 military service. From 1919 until his death - taught at the Academy in Breslau. In this period, numerous trips to the Balkans.

GABRIELE MÜNTER

Born 19.2.1877 in Berlin, died 19.2.1962 in Murnau. 1897 art classes at an art school for ladies in Düsseldorf. 1901 art studies in Munich. 1902 studied at the "Phalanx" Art School under Kandinsky. From 1904-08, travelled through Europe and North Africa with Kandinsky. 1908 co-founder of the "New Artists' Association of Munich". Joined the "Blue Rider" Group. 1914-20 journeyed through Scandinavia. 1916 separation from Kandinsky, who had left Germany at the outbreak of war. 1920

returned to Germany. 1929-30 stayed in France. Resident in Murnau from 1931. 1956 Cultural Prize of Munich.

EMIL NOLDE

Born 7.8.1867 in Nolde (Schleswig), died 13.4. 1956 in Seebüll. 1884-88 apprenticeship as woodcarver in Flensburg. 1889 studied at the School of Arts and Crafts in Karlsruhe. Taught from 1892-98 at the School of Crafts in St Gallen. 1898, studied at a private art school in Munich. 1899, student of Hoelzel in Dachau, subsequently at the Academie Julian in Paris. In the years following in Copenhagen and Berlin. Settled on the island of Alsen in 1903. Resident in Berlin from 1906, but continued to spend the summer months on Alsen. 1906-07 member of the Artists' Group "Die Brücke". 1910 member of the "New Secession" in Berlin. 1911 journeyed to Holland, meeting with Ensor. 1913-14 took part in an ethnological expedition to the South Seas and the Far East. After the War, lived in Berlin and Seebüll. 1931 Member of the Prussian Academy of the Arts. Denounced as "degenerate" by the National Socialists. 1937 his works confiscated. 1941 prohibited from painting. 1942, his atelier in Berlin destroyed by bombing. 1946 appointed professor. 1950 awarded a prize at the Biennale in Venice.

MAX PECHSTEIN

Born 31.12.1881 in Zwickau, died 19.6.1955 in Berlin. After completing an apprenticeship as a painter, was at the School of Arts and Crafts in Dresden from 1900. 1902-06, studied at the Academy there.

1906 member of the Artists' Group "Die Brücke". 1907, journeyed to Italy and Paris. Resident in Berlin from 1908. Co-founder and president of the New Secession. 1913-14 journeyed to Palau in the Pacific, becoming a Japanese prisoner of war at the outbreak of war. 1915 succeeded in returning to Germany. 1916-17 military service. 1919 in Berlin again. 1923 appointed to the Berlin Academy. Removed from office by the National Socialists, prohibited from painting or exhibiting. 1944-45, military service in Pomerania, briefly Russian prisoner of war. 1945 taught again at the Berlin Academy, 1951 honorary senator there. 1952 award of the Order of the FRG, 1954 Art Prize of the City of Berlin.

CHRISTIAN ROHLFS

Born 22.12.1849 in Niendorf (Holstein), died 8.1.1938 in Hagen. 1870 studied at the Art School in Weimar. After a long illness, amputation of one leg. 1874 in Weimar again. 1877 first exhibition. 1910 appointment to the Folkwang School in Hagen by Karl Ernst Osthaus. Moved to Hagen. Spent the summer months 1905-06 in Soest, meeting with Nolde. Took part in the exhibition of the Sonderbund in Düsseldorf and member of the Berlin Secession. 1910-12 sojourned in Munich and in the Tyrol. 1911 member of the New Secession in Berlin. 1912 in Hagen again. 1922 award of doctorate in engineering by the Technical University in Aachen. 1924 Freeman of the City of Hagen, member of the Prussian Academy of Graphic Arts. 1925 awarded an honorary Ph.D. by the University of Kiel. From 1927 lived alternately in Hagen and Ascona. 1929 foundation of the Christian Rohlfs

Museum in Hagen. 1937 excluded from the Prussian Academy by the National Socialists and denounced as being "degenerate".

KARL SCHMIDT-ROTTLUFF

Born 1.12.1884 in Rottluff near Chemnitz (=Karl Marx Stadt), died 10.8.1976 in Berlin. 1905-07 studied architecture at the Technical University of Dresden. Co-founder of the Artists' Group "Die Brücke". 1906 on the island of Alsen with Nolde. In the summer months from 1907-12, he worked in Dangast on the North Sea. One-man shows in Braunschweig 1907 and Hamburg 1910. Resident in Berlin from 1911. 1912 took part in the Sonderbund exhibition in Cologne. 1915-18 military service. Until 1930, various journeys through the Mediterranean countries, longer stays in Paris and Rome. 1931 member of the Prussian Academy of the Graphic Arts. 1933 excluded from this by the National Socialists. 1938 confiscation of his works, 1941 prohibited from painting. 1947 appointment to the Berlin Academy. 1956 awarded the "pour le mérite" medal for assistance with the founding of the "Brücke" Museum in Berlin. 1970 Freeman of the City of Berlin.